EUGÈNE IONESCO: *Four Plays*

The Bald Soprano
The Lesson
Jack, or The Submission
The Chairs

Works by Eugène Ionesco
Published by Grove Weidenfeld

Exit the King, The Killer, *and* Macbett

Four Plays (The Bald Soprano; The Lesson; The Chairs; Jack, or The Submission)

Hugoliad: Or The Grotesque and Tragic Life of Victor Hugo

Man with Bags

Present Past, Past Present

Rhinoceros and Other Plays (The Leader; The Future Is in Eggs or It Takes All Kinds to Make a World)

Three Plays (Amédée; The New Tenant; Victims of Duty)

EUGÈNE IONESCO

FOUR PLAYS

•

The Bald Soprano

The Lesson

Jack, or The Submission

The Chairs

•

Translated by Donald M. Allen

GROVE WEIDENFELD • NEW YORK

Published by Grove Weidenfeld
A division of Wheatland Corporation
841 Broadway
New York, NY 10003-4793

The French texts of these plays were originally published in France in *Eugène Ionesco: Théâtre,* Volume I, copyright by Librairie Gallimard, 1954. A shortened version of the translation of *The Bald Soprano* was published in *New World Writing, Ninth Mentor Selection,* copyright © 1956, by Eugène Ionesco.

Library of Congress Catalog Card Number: 58-7344
ISBN 0-8021-3079-8

Manufactured in the United States of America

Printed on acid-free paper

First Evergreen Edition 1982

55 54 53 52 51 50 49

Contents

A NOTE ON THE ORIGINAL PRODUCTIONS

La Cantatrice chauve was first produced at the Théâtre des Noctambules, on May 11, 1950, by a company of young actors which included Paulette Frantz, Simone Mozet, Odette Barrois, Nicolas Bataille, Claude Mansard and Henry-Jacques Huet.

•

La Leçon was first produced at the Théâtre de Poche, February 20, 1951. The role of the Professor was played by Marcel Cuvelier, the Pupil by Rosette Zuchelli, and the Maid by Claude Mansard.

•

Jacques ou la soumission was first produced in October, 1955, at the Théâtre de la Huchette. Robert Postec directed the play. The role of Jack was played by Jean-Louis Trintignant and that of Roberta by Reine Courtois; other parts were taken by Tsilla Chelton, Madeleine Damien, Paulette Frantz, Pierre Leproux, Claude Mansard, and Claude Thibault. The stage set, costumes and mask were designed by Jacques Noël.

•

Les Chaises was produced for the first time on April 22, 1952, at the Théâtre Lancry. It was directed by Sylvain Dhomme, who played the Orator, and the set was designed by Jacques Noël. The roles of the old people were played by Tsilla Chelton and Paul Chevalier. The play was revived in 1956, at the Studio des Champs Elysées, under the direction of Jacques Mauclair, who played the role of the Old Man.

THE BALD SOPRANO

•

Anti-play

The Characters

Mr. Smith
Mrs. Smith
Mr. Martin
Mrs. Martin
Mary, *the maid*
The Fire Chief

Scene: *A middle-class English interior, with English armchairs. An English evening. Mr. Smith, an Englishman, seated in his English armchair and wearing English slippers, is smoking his English pipe and reading an English newspaper, near an English fire. He is wearing English spectacles and a small gray English mustache. Beside him, in another English armchair, Mrs. Smith, an Englishwoman, is darning some English socks. A long moment of English silence. The English clock strikes 17 English strokes.*

MRS. SMITH: There, it's nine o'clock. We've drunk the soup, and eaten the fish and chips, and the English salad. The children have drunk English water. We've eaten well this evening. That's because we live in the suburbs of London and because our name is Smith.

MR. SMITH [*continues to read, clicks his tongue.*]

MRS. SMITH: Potatoes are very good fried in fat; the salad oil was not rancid. The oil from the grocer at the corner is better quality than the oil from the grocer across the street. It is even better than the oil from the grocer at the bottom of the street. However, I prefer not to tell them that their oil is bad.

MR. SMITH [*continues to read, clicks his tongue.*]

MRS. SMITH: However, the oil from the grocer at the corner is still the best.

MR. SMITH [*continues to read, clicks his tongue.*]

MRS. SMITH: Mary did the potatoes very well, this evening. The last time she did not do them well. I do not like them when they are well done.

MR. SMITH [*continues to read, clicks his tongue.*]

MRS. SMITH: The fish was fresh. It made my mouth water. I had two helpings. No, three helpings. That made me go to the w.c. You also had three helpings. However, the third time you took less than the first two times, while as for me, I took a great deal more. I eat better than you this evening. Why is that? Usually, it is you who eats more. It is not appetite you lack.

MR. SMITH [*clicks his tongue.*]

MRS. SMITH: But still, the soup was perhaps a little too salt. It was saltier than you. Ha, ha, ha. It also had too many leeks and not enough onions. I regret I didn't advise Mary to add some aniseed stars. The next time I'll know better.

MR. SMITH [*continues to read, clicks his tongue.*]

MRS. SMITH: Our little boy wanted to drink some beer; he's going to love getting tiddly. He's like you. At table did you notice how he stared at the bottle? But I poured some water from the jug into his glass. He was thirsty and he drank it. Helen is like me: she's a good manager, thrifty, plays the piano. She never asks to drink English beer. She's like our little daughter who drinks only milk and eats only porridge. It's obvious that she's only two. She's named Peggy. The quince and bean pie was marvelous. It would have been nice, perhaps, to have had a small glass of Australian Burgundy with the sweet, but I did not bring the bottle to the table because I did not wish to set the children a bad example of gluttony. They must learn to be sober and temperate.

MR. SMITH [*continues to read, clicks his tongue.*]

MRS. SMITH: Mrs. Parker knows a Rumanian grocer by the name of Popesco Rosenfeld, who has just come from Constantinople. He is a great specialist in yogurt. He has a diploma from the school of yogurt-making in Adrianople. Tomorrow I shall buy a large pot of native Rumanian yogurt from him. One doesn't often find such things here in the suburbs of London.

MR. SMITH [*continues to read, clicks his tongue.*]

MRS. SMITH: Yogurt is excellent for the stomach, the kidneys, the appendicitis, and apotheosis. It was Doctor Mackenzie-King who told me that, he's the one who takes care of the children of our neighbors, the Johns. He's a good doctor. One can trust him. He never prescribes any medicine that he's not tried out on himself first. Before operating on Parker, he had his own liver operated on first, although he was not the least bit ill.

MR. SMITH: But how does it happen that the doctor pulled through while Parker died?

MRS. SMITH: Because the operation was successful in the doctor's case and it was not in Parker's.

MR. SMITH: Then Mackenzie is not a good doctor. The operation should have succeeded with both of them or else both should have died.

MRS. SMITH: Why?

MR. SMITH: A conscientious doctor must die with his patient if they can't get well together. The captain of a ship goes down with his ship into the briny deep, he does not survive alone.

MRS. SMITH: One cannot compare a patient with a ship.

MR. SMITH: Why not? A ship has its diseases too; moreover, your doctor is as hale as a ship; that's why he should have perished at the same time as his patient, like the captain and his ship.

MRS. SMITH: Ah! I hadn't thought of that . . . Perhaps it is true . . . And then, what conclusion do you draw from this?

MR. SMITH: All doctors are quacks. And all patients too. Only the Royal Navy is honest in England.

MRS. SMITH: But not sailors.

MR. SMITH: Naturally [*A pause. Still reading his paper*:] Here's a thing I don't understand. In the newspaper they always give the age of deceased persons but never the age of the newly born. That doesn't make sense.

MRS. SMITH: I never thought of that!

[*Another moment of silence. The clock strikes seven times. Silence. The clock strikes three times. Silence. The clock doesn't strike.*]

MR. SMITH [*still reading his paper*]: Tsk, it says here that Bobby Watson died.

MRS. SMITH: My God, the poor man! When did he die?

MR. SMITH: Why do you pretend to be astonished? You know very well that he's been dead these past two years. Surely you remember that we attended his funeral a year and a half ago.

MRS. SMITH:Oh yes, of course I do remember. I remembered it right away, but I don't understand why you yourself were so surprised to see it in the paper.

MR. SMITH: It wasn't in the paper. It's been three years since his death was announced. I remembered it through an association of ideas.

MRS. SMITH: What a pity! He was so well preserved.

MR. SMITH: He was the handsomest corpse in Great Britain. He didn't look his age. Poor Bobby, he'd been dead for four years and he was still warm. A veritable living corpse. And how cheerful he was!

MRS. SMITH: Poor Bobby.

MR. SMITH: Which poor Bobby do you mean?

MRS. SMITH: It is his wife that I mean. She is called Bobby too, Bobby Watson. Since they both had the same name, you could never tell one from the other when you saw them together. It was only after his death that you could really tell which was which. And there are still people today who confuse her with the deceased and offer their condolences to him. Do you know her?

MR. SMITH: I only met her once, by chance, at Bobby's burial.

MRS. SMITH: I've never seen her. Is she pretty?

MR. SMITH: She has regular features and yet one cannot say that she is pretty. She is too big and stout. Her features are not regular but still one can say that she is very pretty. She is a little too small and too thin. She's a voice teacher.

[*The clock strikes five times. A long silence.*]

MRS. SMITH: And when do they plan to be married, those two?

MR. SMITH: Next spring, at the latest.

MRS. SMITH: We shall have to go to their wedding, I suppose.

MR. SMITH: We shall have to give them a wedding present. I wonder what?

MRS. SMITH: Why don't we give them one of the seven silver salvers that were given us for our wedding and which have never been of any use to us? [*Silence.*]

MRS. SMITH: How sad for her to be left a widow so young.

MR. SMITH: Fortunately, they had no children.

MRS. SMITH: That was all they needed! Children! Poor woman, how could she have managed!

MR. SMITH: She's still young. She might very well remarry. She looks so well in mourning.

MRS. SMITH: But who would take care of the children? You

know very well that they have a boy and a girl. What are their names?

MR. SMITH: Bobby and Bobby like their parents. Bobby Watson's uncle, old Bobby Watson, is a rich man and very fond of the boy. He might very well pay for Bobby's education.

MRS. SMITH: That would be proper. And Bobby Watson's aunt, old Bobby Watson, might very well, in her turn, pay for the education of Bobby Watson, Bobby Watson's daughter. That way Bobby, Bobby Watson's mother, could remarry. Has she anyone in mind?

MR. SMITH: Yes, a cousin of Bobby Watson's.

MRS. SMITH: Who? Bobby Watson?

MR. SMITH: Which Bobby Watson do you mean?

MRS. SMITH: Why, Bobby Watson, the son of old Bobby Watson, the late Bobby Watson's other uncle.

MR. SMITH: No, it's not that one, it's someone else. It's Bobby Watson, the son of old Bobby Watson, the late Bobby Watson's aunt.

MRS. SMITH: Are you referring to Bobby Watson the commercial traveler?

MR. SMITH: All the Bobby Watsons are commercial travelers.

MRS. SMITH: What a difficult trade! However, they do well at it.

MR. SMITH: Yes, when there's no competition.

MRS. SMITH: And when is there no competition?

MR. SMITH: On Tuesdays, Thursdays, and Tuesdays.

MRS. SMITH: Ah! Three days a week? And what does Bobby Watson do on those days?

MR. SMITH: He rests, he sleeps.

MRS. SMITH: But why doesn't he work those three days if there's no competition?

MR. SMITH: I don't know everything. I can't answer all your idiotic questions!

MRS. SMITH [*offended*]: Oh! Are you trying to humiliate me?

MR. SMITH [*all smiles*]: You know very well that I'm not.

MRS. SMITH: Men are all alike! You sit there all day long, a cigarette in your mouth, or you powder your nose and rouge your lips, fifty times a day, or else you drink like a fish.

MR. SMITH: But what would you say if you saw men acting like women do, smoking all day long, powdering, rouging their lips, drinking whisky?

MRS. SMITH: It's nothing to me! But if you're only saying that to annoy me . . . I don't care for that kind of joking, you know that very well!

[*She hurls the socks across the stage and shows her teeth. She gets up.**]

MR. SMITH [*also getting up and going towards his wife, tenderly*]: Oh, my little ducky daddles, what a little spitfire you are! You know that I only said it as a joke! [*He takes her by the waist and kisses her.*] What a ridiculous pair of old lovers we are! Come, let's put out the lights and go bye-byes.

MARY [*entering*]: I'm the maid. I have spent a very pleasant afternoon. I've been to the cinema with a man and I've seen a film with some women. After the cinema, we went to drink some brandy and milk and then read the newspaper.

MRS. SMITH: I hope that you've spent a pleasant afternoon, that you went to the cinema with a man and that you drank some brandy and milk.

MR. SMITH: And the newspaper.

MARY: Mr. and Mrs. Martin, your guests, are at the door. They were waiting for me. They didn't dare come in by themselves. They were supposed to have dinner with you this evening.

MRS. SMITH: Oh, yes. We were expecting them. And we were hungry. Since they didn't put in an appearance, we were going to start dinner without them. We've had nothing to eat all day. You should not have gone out!

MARY: But it was you who gave me permission.

MR. SMITH: We didn't do it on purpose.

* In Nicolas Bataille's production, Mrs. Smith did not show her teeth, nor did she throw the socks very far.

MARY [*bursts into laughter, then she bursts into tears. Then she smiles*]: I bought me a chamber pot.

MRS. SMITH: My dear Mary, please open the door and ask Mr. and Mrs. Martin to step in. We will change quickly.

[*Mr. and Mrs. Smith exit right. Mary opens the door at the left by which Mr. and Mrs. Martin enter.*]

MARY: Why have you come so late! You are not very polite. People should be punctual. Do you understand? But sit down there, anyway, and wait now that you're here.

[*She exits. Mr. and Mrs. Martin sit facing each other, without speaking. They smile timidly at each other. The dialogue which follows must be spoken in voices that are drawling, monotonous, a little singsong, without nuances.**]

MR. MARTIN: Excuse me, madam, but it seems to me, unless I'm mistaken, that I've met you somewhere before.

MRS. MARTIN: I, too, sir. It seems to me that I've met you somewhere before.

MR. MARTIN: Was it, by any chance, at Manchester that I caught a glimpse of you, madam?

MRS. MARTIN: That is very possible. I am originally from the city of Manchester. But I do not have a good memory, sir. I cannot say whether it was there that I caught a glimpse of you or not!

MR. MARTIN: Good God, that's curious! I, too, am originally from the city of Manchester, madam!

MRS. MARTIN: That is curious!

MR. MARTIN: Isn't that curious! Only, I, madam, I left the city of Manchester about five weeks ago.

MRS. MARTIN: That is curious! What a bizarre coincidence! I, too, sir, I left the city of Manchester about five weeks ago.

MR. MARTIN: Madam, I took the 8:30 morning train which arrives in London at 4:45.

MRS. MARTIN: That is curious! How very bizarre! And what a coincidence! I took the same train, sir, I too.

MR. MARTIN: Good Lord, how curious! Perhaps then, madam,

* In Nicolas Bataille's production, this dialogue was spoken in a tone and played in a style sincerely tragic.

it was on the train that I saw you?

MRS. MARTIN: It is indeed possible; that is, not unlikely. It is plausible and, after all, why not!—But I don't recall it, sir!

MR. MARTIN: I traveled second class, madam. There is no second class in England, but I always travel second class.

MRS. MARTIN: That is curious! How very bizarre! And what a coincidence! I, too, sir, I traveled second class.

MR. MARTIN: How curious that is! Perhaps we did meet in second class, my dear lady!

MRS. MARTIN: That is certainly possible, and it is not at all unlikely. But I do not remember very well, my dear sir!

MR. MARTIN: My seat was in coach No. 8, compartment 6, my dear lady.

MRS. MARTIN: How curious that is! My seat was also in coach No. 8, compartment 6, my dear sir!

MR. MARTIN: How curious that is and what a bizarre coincidence! Perhaps we met in compartment 6, my dear lady?

MRS. MARTIN: It is indeed possible, after all! But I do not recall it, my dear sir!

MR. MARTIN: To tell the truth, my dear lady, I do not remember it either, but it is possible that we caught a glimpse of each other there, and as I think of it, it seems to me even very likely.

MRS. MARTIN: Oh! truly, of course, truly, sir!

MR. MARTIN: How curious it is! I had seat No. 3, next to the window, my dear lady.

MRS. MARTIN: Oh, good Lord, how curious and bizarre! I had seat No. 6, next to the window, across from you, my dear sir.

MR. MARTIN: Good God, how curious that is and what a coincidence! We were then seated facing each other, my dear lady! It is there that we must have seen each other!

MRS. MARTIN: How curious it is! It is possible, but I do not recall it, sir!

MR. MARTIN: To tell the truth, my dear lady, I do not remember it either. However, it is very possible that we saw each other on that occasion.

MRS. MARTIN: It is true, but I am not at all sure of it, sir.

MR. MARTIN: Dear madam, were you not the lady who asked me to place her suitcase in the luggage rack and who thanked me and gave me permission to smoke?

MRS. MARTIN: But of course, that must have been I, sir. How curious it is, how curious it is, and what a coincidence!

MR. MARTIN: How curious it is, how bizarre, what a coincidence! And well, well, it was perhaps at that moment that we came to know each other, madam?

MRS. MARTIN: How curious it is and what a coincidence! It is indeed possible, my dear sir! However, I do not believe that I recall it.

MR. MARTIN: Nor do I, madam. [*A moment of silence. The clock strikes twice, then once.*] Since coming to London, I have resided in Bromfield Street, my dear lady.

MRS. MARTIN: How curious that is, how bizarre! I, too, since coming to London, I have resided in Bromfield Street, my dear sir.

MR. MARTIN: How curious that is, well then, well then, perhaps we have seen each other in Bromfield Street, my dear lady.

MRS. MARTIN: How curious that is, how bizarre! It is indeed possible, after all! But I do not recall it, my dear sir.

MR. MARTIN: I reside at No. 19, my dear lady.

MRS. MARTIN: How curious that is. I also reside at No. 19, my dear sir.

MR. MARTIN: Well then, well then, well then, well then, perhaps we have seen each other in that house, dear lady?

MRS. MARTIN: It is indeed possible but I do not recall it, dear sir.

MR. MARTIN: My flat is on the fifth floor, No. 8, my dear lady.

MRS. MARTIN: How curious it is, good Lord, how bizarre! And what a coincidence! I too reside on the fifth floor, in flat No. 8, dear sir!

MR. MARTIN [*musing*]: How curious it is, how curious it is, how curious it is, and what a coincidence! You know, in my bedroom there is a bed, and it is covered with a green eiderdown. This room, with the bed and the green eiderdown, is at the end of the corridor between the w.c. and the bookcase, dear lady!

MRS. MARTIN: What a coincidence, good Lord, what a coincidence! My bedroom, too, has a bed with a green eiderdown and is at the end of the corridor, between the w.c., dear sir, and the bookcase!

MR. MARTIN: How bizarre, curious, strange! Then, madam, we live in the same room and we sleep in the same bed, dear lady. It is perhaps there that we have met!

MRS. MARTIN: How curious it is and what a coincidence! It is indeed possible that we have met there, and perhaps even last night. But I do not recall it, dear sir!

MR. MARTIN: I have a little girl, my little daughter, she lives with me, dear lady. She is two years old, she's blonde, she has a white eye and a red eye, she is very pretty, her name is Alice, dear lady.

MRS. MARTIN: What a bizarre coincidence! I, too, have a little girl. She is two years old, has a white eye and a red eye, she is very pretty, and her name is Alice, too, dear sir!

MR. MARTIN [*in the same drawling, nonotonous voice*]: How curious it is and what a coincidence! And bizarre! Perhaps they are the same, dear lady!

MRS. MARTIN: How curious it is! It is indeed possible, dear sir. [*A rather long moment of silence. The clock strikes 29 times.*]

MR. MARTIN [*after having reflected at length, gets up slowly and, unhurriedly, moves toward Mrs. Martin, who, surprised by his solemn air, has also gotten up very quietly. Mr. Martin, in the same flat, monotonous voice, slightly singsong*]: Then, dear lady, I believe that there can be no doubt about it, we have seen each other before and you are my own wife . . . Elizabeth, I have found you again!

[*Mrs. Martin approaches Mr. Martin without haste. They embrace without expression. The clock strikes once, very loud. This striking of the clock must be so loud that it makes the audience jump. The Martins do not hear it.*]

MRS. MARTIN: Donald, it's you, darling!

[*They sit together in the same armchair, their arms around each other, and fall asleep. The clock strikes several more times. Mary, on tiptoe, a finger to her lips, enters quietly and addresses the audience.*]

MARY: Elizabeth and Donald are now too happy to be able to hear me. I can therefore let you in on a secret. Elizabeth is not Elizabeth, Donald is not Donald. And here is the proof: the child that Donald spoke of is not Elizabeth's daughter, they are not the same person. Donald's daughter has one white eye and one red eye like Elizabeth's daughter. Whereas Donald's child has a white right eye and a red left eye, Elizabeth's child has a red right eye and a white left eye! Thus all of Donald's system of deduction collapses when it comes up against this last obstacle which destroys his whole theory. In spite of the extraordinary coincidences which seem to be definitive proofs, Donald and Elizabeth, not being the parents of the same child, are not Donald and Elizabeth. It is in vain that he thinks he is Donald, it is in vain that she thinks she is Elizabeth. He believes in vain that she is Elizabeth. She believes in vain that he is Donald —they are sadly deceived. But who is the true Donald? Who is the true Elizabeth? Who has any interest in prolonging this confusion? I don't know. Let's not try to know. Let's leave things as they are. [*She takes several steps toward the door, then returns and says to the audience:*] My real name is Sherlock Holmes. [*She exits.*]

[*The clock strikes as much as it likes. After several seconds, Mr. and Mrs. Martin separate and take the chairs they had at the beginning.*]

MR. MARTIN: Darling, let's forget all that has not passed between us, and, now that we have found each other again, let's try not to lose each other any more, and live as before.

MRS. MARTIN: Yes, darling.

[*Mr. and Mrs. Smith enter from the right, wearing the same clothes.*]

MRS. SMITH: Good evening, dear friends! Please forgive us for having made you wait so long. We thought that we should extend you the courtesy to which you are entitled and as soon as we learned that you had been kind enough to give us the pleasure of coming to see us without prior notice we hurried to dress for the occasion.

MR. SMITH [*furious*]: We've had nothing to eat all day. And we've been waiting four whole hours for you. Why have you come so late?

[*Mr. and Mrs. Smith sit facing their guests. The striking of the clock underlines the speeches, more or less strongly, according to the case. The Martins, particularly Mrs. Martin, seem embarrassed and timid. For this reason the conversation begins with difficulty and the words are uttered, at the beginning, awkwardly. A long embarrassed silence at first, then other silences and hesitations follow.*]

MR. SMITH: Hm. [*Silence.*]

MRS. SMITH: Hm, hm. [*Silence.*]

MRS. MARTIN: Hm, hm, hm. [*Silence.*]

MR. MARTIN: Hm, hm, hm, hm. [*Silence.*]

MRS. MARTIN: Oh, but definitely. [*Silence.*]

MR. MARTIN: We all have colds. [*Silence.*]

MR. SMITH: Nevertheless, it's not chilly. [*Silence.*]

MRS. SMITH: There's no draft. [*Silence.*]

MR. MARTIN: Oh no, fortunately. [*Silence.*]

MR. SMITH: Oh dear, oh dear, oh dear. [*Silence.*]

MR. MARTIN: Don't you feel well? [*Silence.*]

MRS. SMITH: No, he's wet his pants. [*Silence.*]

MRS. MARTIN: Oh, sir, at your age, you shouldn't. [*Silence.*]

MR. SMITH: The heart is ageless. [*Silence.*]

MR. MARTIN: That's true. [*Silence.*]

MRS. SMITH: So they say. [*Silence.*]

MRS. MARTIN: They also say the opposite. [*Silence.*]

MR. SMITH: The truth lies somewhere between the two. [*Silence.*]

MR. MARTIN: That's true. [*Silence.*]

MRS. SMITH [*to the Martins*]: Since you travel so much, you must have many interesting things to tell us.

MR. MARTIN [*to his wife*]: My dear, tell us what you've seen today.

MRS. MARTIN: It's scarcely worth the trouble, for no one would believe me.

MR. SMITH: We're not going to question your sincerity!

MRS. SMITH: You will offend us if you think that.

MR. MARTIN [*to his wife*]: You will offend them, my dear, if you think that . . .

MRS. MARTIN [*graciously*]: Oh well, today I witnessed something extraordinary. Something really incredible.

MR. MARTIN: Tell us quickly, my dear.

MR. SMITH: Oh, this is going to be amusing.

MRS. SMITH: At last.

MRS. MARTIN: Well, today, when I went shopping to buy some vegetables, which are getting to be dearer and dearer . . .

MRS. SMITH: Where is it all going to end!

MR. SMITH: You shouldn't interrupt, my dear, it's very rude.

MRS. MARTIN: In the street, near a café, I saw a man, properly dressed, about fifty years old, or not even that, who . . .

MR. SMITH: Who, what?

MRS. SMITH: Who, what?

MR. SMITH [*to his wife*]: Don't interrupt, my dear, you're disgusting.

MRS. SMITH: My dear, it is you who interrupted first, you boor.

MR. SMITH [*to his wife*]: Hush. [*To Mrs. Martin*:] What was this man doing?

MRS. MARTIN: Well, I'm sure you'll say that I'm making it up—he was down on one knee and he was bent over.

MR. MARTIN, MR. SMITH, MRS. SMITH: Oh!

MRS. MARTIN: Yes, bent over.

MR. SMITH: Not possible.

MRS. MARTIN: Yes, bent over. I went near him to see what he was doing . . .

MR. SMITH: And?

MRS. MARTIN: He was tying his shoe lace which had come undone.

MR. MARTIN, MR. SMITH, MRS. SMITH: Fantastic!

MR. SMITH: If someone else had told me this, I'd not believe it.

MR. MARTIN: Why not? One sees things even more extraordinary every day, when one walks around. For instance, today in the Underground I myself saw a man, quietly sitting on a seat, reading his newspaper.

MRS. SMITH: What a character!

MR. SMITH: Perhaps it was the same man!

[*The doorbell rings.*]

MR. SMITH: Goodness, someone is ringing.

MRS. SMITH: There must be somebody there. I'll go and see. [*She goes to see, she opens the door and closes it, and comes back.*] Nobody. [*She sits down again.*]

MR. MARTIN: I'm going to give you another example . . .

[*Doorbell rings again.*]

MR. SMITH: Goodness, someone is ringing.

MRS. SMITH: There must be somebody there. I'll go and see. [*She goes to see, opens the door, and comes back.*] No one. [*She sits down again.*]

MR. MARTIN [*who has forgotten where he was*]: Uh . . .

MRS. MARTIN: You were saying that you were going to give us another example.

MR. MARTIN: Oh, yes . . .

[*Doorbell rings again.*]

MR. SMITH: Goodness, someone is ringing.

MRS. SMITH: I'm not going to open the door again.

MR. SMITH: Yes, but there must be someone there!

MRS. SMITH: The first time there was no one. The second time, no one. Why do you think that there is someone there now?

MR. SMITH: Because someone has rung!

MRS. MARTIN: That's no reason.

MR. MARTIN: What? When one hears the doorbell ring, that means someone is at the door ringing to have the door opened.

MRS. MARTIN: Not always. You've just seen otherwise!

MR. MARTIN: In most cases, yes.

MR. SMITH: As for me, when I go to visit someone, I ring in order to be admitted. I think that everyone does the same thing and that each time there is a ring there must be someone there.

MRS. SMITH: That is true in theory. But in reality things happen differently. You have just seen otherwise.

MRS. MARTIN: Your wife is right.

MR. MARTIN: Oh! You women! You always stand up for each other.

MRS. SMITH: Well, I'll go and see. You can't say that I am obstinate, but you will see that there's no one there! [*She goes to look, opens the door and closes it.*] You see, there's no one there. [*She returns to her seat.*]

MRS. SMITH: Oh, these men who always think they're right and who're always wrong!

[*The doorbell rings again.*]

MR. SMITH: Goodness, someone is ringing. There must be someone there.

MRS. SMITH [*in a fit of anger*]: Don't send me to open the door again. You've seen that it was useless. Experience teaches us that when one hears the doorbell ring it is because there is never anyone there.

MRS. MARTIN: Never.

MR. MARTIN: That's not entirely accurate.

MR. SMITH: In fact it's false. When one hears the doorbell ring it is because there is someone there.

MRS. SMITH: He won't admit he's wrong.

MRS. MARTIN: My husband is very obstinate, too.

MR. SMITH: There's someone there.

MR. MARTIN: That's not impossible.

MRS. SMITH [*to her husband*]: No.

MR. SMITH: Yes.

MRS. SMITH: I tell you *no*. In any case you are not going to disturb me again for nothing. If you wish to know, go and look yourself!

MR. SMITH: I'll go.

[*Mrs. Smith shrugs her shoulders. Mrs. Martin tosses her head.*]

MR. SMITH [*opening the door*]: Oh! how do you do. [*He glances at Mrs. Smith and the Martins, who are all surprise.*] It's the Fire Chief!

FIRE CHIEF [*he is of course in uniform and is wearing an enormous shining helmet*]: Good evening, ladies and gentlemen. [*The Smiths and the Martins are still slightly astonished. Mrs. Smith turns her head away, in a temper, and does not reply to his greeting.*] Good evening, Mrs. Smith. You appear to be angry.

MRS. SMITH: Oh!

MR. SMITH: You see it's because my wife is a little chagrined at having been proved wrong.

MR. MARTIN: There's been an argument between Mr. and Mrs. Smith, Mr. Fire Chief.

MRS. SMITH [*to Mr. Martin*]: This is no business of yours! [*To Mr. Smith*:] I beg you not to involve outsiders in our family arguments.

MR. SMITH: Oh, my dear, this is not so serious. The Fire Chief is an old friend of the family. His mother courted me, and I knew his father. He asked me to give him my daughter in marriage if ever I had one. And he died waiting.

MR. MARTIN: That's neither his fault, nor yours.

FIRE CHIEF: Well, what is it all about?

MRS. SMITH: My husband was claiming . . .

MR. SMITH: No, it was you who was claiming.

MR. MARTIN: Yes, it was she.

MRS. MARTIN: No, it was he.

FIRE CHIEF: Don't get excited. You tell me, Mrs. Smith.

MRS. SMITH: Well, this is how it was. It is difficult for me to speak openly to you, but a fireman is also a confessor.

FIRE CHIEF: Well then?

MRS. SMITH: We were arguing because my husband said that each time the doorbell rings there is always someone there.

MR. MARTIN: It is plausible.

MRS. SMITH: And I was saying that each time the doorbell rings there is never anyone there.

MRS. MARTIN: It might seem strange.

MRS. SMITH: But it has been proved, not by theoretical demonstrations, but by facts.

MR. SMITH: That's false, since the Fire Chief is here. He rang the bell, I opened the door, and there he was.

MRS. MARTIN: When?

MR. MARTIN: But just now.

MRS. SMITH: Yes, but it was only when you heard the doorbell ring the fourth time that there was someone there. And the fourth time does not count.

MRS. MARTIN: Never. It is only the first three times that count.

MR. SMITH: Mr. Fire Chief, permit me in my turn to ask you several questions.

FIRE CHIEF: Go right ahead.

MR. SMITH: When I opened the door and saw you, it was really you who had rung the bell?

FIRE CHIEF: Yes, it was I.

MR. MARTIN: You were at the door? And you rang in order to be admitted?

FIRE CHIEF: I do not deny it.

MR. SMITH [*to his wife, triumphantly*]: You see? I was right. When you hear the doorbell ring, that means someone rang it. You certainly cannot say that the Fire Chief is not someone.

MRS. SMITH: Certainly not. I repeat to you that I was speaking of only the first three times, since the fourth time does not count.

MRS. MARTIN: And when the doorbell rang the first time, was it you?

FIRE CHIEF: No, it was not I.

MRS. MARTIN: You see? The doorbell rang and there was no one there.

MR. MARTIN: Perhaps it was someone else?

MR. SMITH: Were you standing at the door for a long time?

FIRE CHIEF: Three-quarters of an hour.

MR. SMITH: And you saw no one?

FIRE CHIEF: No one. I am sure of that.

MRS. MARTIN: And did you hear the bell when it rang the second time?

FIRE CHIEF: Yes, and that wasn't I either. And there was still no one there.

MRS. SMITH: Victory! I was right.

MR. SMITH [*to his wife*]: Not so fast. [*To the Fire Chief*:] And what were you doing at the door?

FIRE CHIEF: Nothing. I was just standing there. I was thinking of many things.

MR. MARTIN [*to the Fire Chief*]: But the third time—it was not you who rang?

FIRE CHIEF: Yes, it was I.

MR. SMITH: But when the door was opened nobody was in sight.

FIRE CHIEF: That was because I had hidden myself—as a joke.

MRS. SMITH: Don't make jokes, Mr. Fire Chief. This business is too sad.

MR. MARTIN: In short, we still do not know whether, when the doorbell rings, there is someone there or not!

MRS. SMITH: Never anyone.

MR. SMITH: Always someone.

FIRE CHIEF: I am going to reconcile you. You both are partly right. When the doorbell rings, sometimes there is someone, other times there is no one.

MR. MARTIN: This seems logical to me.

MRS. MARTIN: I think so too.

FIRE CHIEF: Life is very simple, really. [*To the Smiths*:] Go on and kiss each other.

MRS. SMITH: We just kissed each other a little while ago.

MR. MARTIN: They'll kiss each other tomorrow. They have plenty of time.

MRS. SMITH: Mr. Fire Chief, since you have helped us settle this, please make yourself comfortable, take off your helmet and sit down for a moment.

FIRE CHIEF: Excuse me, but I can't stay long. I should like to remove my helmet, but I haven't time to sit down. [*He sits down, without removing his helmet.*] I must admit that I have come to see you for another reason. I am on official business.

MRS. SMITH: And what can we do for you, Mr. Fire Chief?

FIRE CHIEF: I must beg you to excuse my indiscretion [*terribly embarrassed*] . . . uhm [*He points a finger at the Martins*] . . . you don't mind . . . in front of them . . .

MRS. MARTIN: Say whatever you like.

MR. MARTIN: We're old friends. They tell us everything.

MR. SMITH: Speak.

FIRE CHIEF: Eh, well—is there a fire here?

MRS. SMITH: Why do you ask us that?

FIRE CHIEF: It's because—pardon me—I have orders to extinguish all the fires in the city.

MRS. MARTIN: All?

FIRE CHIEF: Yes, all.

MRS. SMITH [*confused*]: I don't know . . . I don't think so. Do you want me to go and look?

MR. SMITH [*sniffing*]: There can't be one here. There's no smell of anything burning.*

FIRE CHIEF [*aggrieved*]: None at all? You don't have a little

* In Nicolas Bataille's production Mr. and Mrs. Martin sniffed too.

fire in the chimney, something burning in the attic or in the cellar? A little fire just starting, at least?

MRS. SMITH: I am sorry to disappoint you but I do not believe there's anything here at the moment. I promise that I will notify you when we do have something.

FIRE CHIEF: Please don't forget, it would be a great help.

MRS. SMITH: That's a promise.

FIRE CHIEF [*to the Martins*]: And there's nothing burning at your house either?

MRS. MARTIN: No, unfortunately.

MR. MARTIN [*to the Fire Chief*]: Things aren't going so well just now.

FIRE CHIEF: Very poorly. There's been almost nothing, a few trifles—a chimney, a barn. Nothing important. It doesn't bring in much. And since there are no returns, the profits on output are very meager.

MR. SMITH: Times are bad. That's true all over. It's the same this year with business and agriculture as it is with fires, nothing is prospering.

MR. MARTIN: No wheat, no fires.

FIRE CHIEF: No floods either.

MRS. SMITH: But there is some sugar.

MR. SMITH: That's because it is imported.

MRS. MARTIN: It's harder in the case of fires. The tariffs are too high!

FIRE CHIEF: All the same, there's an occasional asphyxiation by gas, but that's unusual too. For instance, a young woman asphyxiated herself last week—she had left the gas on.

MRS. MARTIN: Had she forgotten it?

FIRE CHIEF: No, but she thought it was her comb.

MR. SMITH: These confusions are always dangerous!

MRS. SMITH: Did you go to see the match dealer?

FIRE CHIEF: There's nothing doing there. He is insured against fires.

MR. MARTIN: Why don't you go see the Vicar of Wakefield, and use my name?

FIRE CHIEF: I don't have the right to extinguish clergymen's fires. The Bishop would get angry. Besides they extinguish their fires themselves, or else they have them put out by vestal virgins.

MR. SMITH: Go see the Durands.

FIRE CHIEF: I can't do that either. He's not English. He's only been naturalized. And naturalized citizens have the right to have houses, but not the right to have them put out if they're burning.

MRS. SMITH: Nevertheless, when they set fire to it last year, it was put out just the same.

FIRE CHIEF: He did that all by himself. Clandestinely. But it's not I who would report him.

MR. SMITH: Neither would I.

MRS. SMITH: Mr. Fire Chief, since you are not too pressed, stay a little while longer. You would be doing us a favor.

FIRE CHIEF: Shall I tell you some stories?

MRS. SMITH: Oh, by all means, how charming of you. [*She kisses him.*]

MR. SMITH, MRS. MARTIN, MR. MARTIN: Yes, yes, some stories, hurrah!

[*They applaud.*]

MR. SMITH: And what is even more interesting is the fact that firemen's stories are all true, and they're based on experience.

FIRE CHIEF: I speak from my own experience. Truth, nothing but the truth. No fiction.

MR. MARTIN: That's right. Truth is never found in books, only in life.

MRS. SMITH: Begin!

MR. MARTIN: Begin!

MRS. MARTIN: Be quiet, he is beginning.

FIRE CHIEF [*coughs slightly several times*]: Excuse me, don't look at me that way. You embarrass me. You know that I am shy.

MRS. SMITH: Isn't he charming! [*she kisses him.*]

FIRE CHIEF: I'm going to try to begin anyhow. But promise me that you won't listen.

MRS. MARTIN: But if we don't listen to you we won't hear you.

FIRE CHIEF: I didn't think of that!

MRS. SMITH: I told you, he's just a boy.

MR. MARTIN, MR. SMITH: Oh, the sweet child! [*They kiss him.**]

MRS. MARTIN: Chin up!

FIRE CHIEF: Well, then! [*He coughs again in a voice shaken by emotion*:] "The Dog and the Cow," an experimental fable. Once upon a time another cow asked another dog: "Why have you not swallowed your trunk?" "Pardon me," replied the dog, "it is because I thought that I was an elephant."

MRS. MARTIN: What is the moral?

FIRE CHIEF: That's for you to find out.

MR. SMITH: He's right.

MRS. SMITH [*furious*]: Tell us another.

FIRE CHIEF: A young calf had eaten too much ground glass. As a result, it was obliged to give birth. It brought forth a cow into the world. However, since the calf was male, the cow could not call him Mamma. Nor could she call him Papa, because the calf was too little. The calf was then obliged to get married and the registry office carried out all the details completely à la mode.

MR. SMITH: À la mode de Caen.

MR. MARTIN: Like tripes.

FIRE CHIEF: You've heard that one?

MRS. SMITH: It was in all the papers.

MRS. MARTIN: It happened not far from our house.

FIRE CHIEF: I'll tell you another: "The Cock." Once upon a time, a cock wished to play the dog. But he had no luck because everyone recognized him right away.

MRS. SMITH: On the other hand, the dog that wished to play

* In Nicolas Bataille's production, they did not kiss the Fire Chief.

the cock was never recognized.

MR. SMITH: I'll tell you one: "The Snake and the Fox." Once upon a time, a snake came up to a fox and said: "It seems to me that I know you!" The fox replied to him: "Me too." "Then," said the snake, "give me some money." "A fox doesn't give money," replied the tricky animal, who, in order to escape, jumped down into a deep ravine full of strawberries and chicken honey. But the snake was there waiting for him with a Mephistophelean laugh. The fox pulled out his knife, shouting: "I'm going to teach you how to live!" Then he took to flight, turning his back. But he had no luck. The snake was quicker. With a well-chosen blow of his fist, he struck the fox in the middle of his forehead, which broke into a thousand pieces, while he cried: "No! No! Four times no! I'm not your daughter."*

MRS. MARTIN: It's interesting.

MRS. SMITH: It's not bad.

MR. MARTIN [*shaking Mr. Smith's hand*]: My congratulations.

FIRE CHIEF [*jealous*]: Not so good. And anyway, I've heard it before.

MR. SMITH: It's terrible.

MRS. SMITH: But it wasn't even true.

MRS. MARTIN: Yes, unfortunately.

MR. MARTIN [*to Mrs. Smith*]: It's your turn, dear lady.

MRS. SMITH: I only know one. I'm going to tell it to you. It's called "The Bouquet."

MR. SMITH: My wife has always been romantic.

MR. MARTIN: She's a true Englishwoman.**

MRS. SMITH: Here it is: Once upon a time, a fiancé gave a bouquet of flowers to his fiancée, who said, "Thanks"; but before she had said, "Thanks," he, without saying a single word, took back the flowers he had given her in order to teach her a good lesson, and he said, "I take them back."

* This story was deleted in Nicolas Bataille's production. Mr. Smith went through the gestures only, without making a sound.

** These two speeches were repeated three times in the original production.

He said, "Goodbye," and took them back and went off in all directions.

MR. MARTIN: Oh, charming! [*He either kisses or does not kiss Mrs. Smith.*]

MRS. MARTIN: You have a wife, Mr. Smith, of whom all the world is jealous.

MR. SMITH: It's true. My wife is intelligence personified. She's even more intelligent than I. In any case, she is much more feminine, everyone says so.

MRS. SMITH [*to the Fire Chief*]: Let's have another, Mr. Fire Chief.

FIRE CHIEF: Oh, no, it's too late.

MR. MARTIN: Tell us one, anyway.

FIRE CHIEF: I'm too tired.

MR. SMITH: Please do us a favor.

MR. MARTIN: I beg you.

FIRE CHIEF: No.

MRS. MARTIN: You have a heart of ice. We're sitting on hot coals.

MRS. SMITH [*falls on her knees sobbing, or else she does not do this*]: I implore you!

FIRE CHIEF: Righto.

MR. SMITH [*in Mrs. Martin's ear*]: He agrees! He's going to bore us again.

MRS. MARTIN: Shh.

MRS. SMITH: No luck. I was too polite.

FIRE CHIEF: "The Headcold." My brother-in law had, on the paternal side, a first cousin whose maternal uncle had a father-in-law whose paternal grandfather had married as his second wife a young native whose brother he had met on one of his travels, a girl of whom he was enamored and by whom he had a son who married an intrepid lady pharmacist who was none other than the niece of an unknown fourth-class petty officer of the Royal Navy and whose adopted father had an aunt who spoke Spanish fluently and who was, perhaps, one of the granddaughters of an engineer who died young, himself the grandson of the owner of a vineyard which produced mediocre wine, but who had a second cousin, a stay-at-home, a sergeant-major, whose son had married a very pretty young woman, a divorcée, whose first husband was the son of a loyal patriot who, in the hope of making his fortune, had managed to bring up one of his daughters so that she could marry a footman who had known Rothschild, and whose brother, after having changed his trade several times, married and had a daughter whose stunted great-grandfather wore spectacles which had been given him by a cousin of his, the brother-in-law of a man from Portugal, natural son of a miller, not too badly off, whose foster-brother had married the daughter of a former country doctor, who was himself a foster-brother of the son of a forrester, himself the natural son of another country doctor, married three times in a row, whose third wife . . .

MR. MARTIN: I knew that third wife, if I'm not mistaken. She ate chicken sitting on a hornet's nest.

FIRE CHIEF: It's not the same one.

MRS. SMITH: Shh!

FIRE CHIEF: As I was saying . . . whose third wife was the daughter of the best midwife in the region and who, early left a widow . . .

MR. SMITH: Like my wife.

FIRE CHIEF: . . . Had married a glazier who was full of life and who had had, by the daughter of a station master, a child who had burned his bridges . . .

MRS. SMITH: His britches?

MR. MARTIN: No his bridge game.

FIRE CHIEF: And had married an oyster woman, whose father had a brother, mayor of a small town, who had taken as his wife a blonde schoolteacher, whose cousin, a fly fisherman . . .

MR. MARTIN: A fly by night?

FIRE CHIEF: . . . Had married another blonde schoolteacher, named Marie, too, whose brother was married to another Marie, also a blonde schoolteacher . . .

MR. SMITH: Since she's blonde, she must be Marie.

FIRE CHIEF: . . . And whose father had been reared in Canada by an old woman who was the niece of a priest whose grandmother, occasionally in the winter, like everyone else, caught a cold.

MRS. SMITH: A curious story. Almost unbelievable.

MR. MARTIN: If you catch a cold, you should get yourself a colt.

MR. SMITH: It's a useless precaution, but alsolutely necessary.

MRS. MARTIN: Excuse me, Mr. Fire Chief, but I did not follow your story very well. At the end, when we got to the grandmother of the priest, I got mixed up.

MR. SMITH: One always gets mixed up in the hands of a priest.

MRS. SMITH: Oh yes, Mr. Fire Chief, begin again. Everyone wants to hear.

FIRE CHIEF: Ah, I don't know whether I'll be able to. I'm on official business. It depends on what time it is.

MRS. SMITH: We don't have the time, here.

FIRE CHIEF: But the clock?

MR. SMITH: It runs badly. It is contradictory, and always indicates the opposite of what the hour really is.

[*Enter Mary*.]

MARY: Madam . . . sir . . .

MRS. SMITH: What do you want?

MR. SMITH: What have you come in here for?

MARY: I hope, madam and sir will excuse me . . . and these ladies and gentlemen too . . . I would like . . . I would like . . . to tell you a story, myself.

MRS. MARTIN: What is she saying?

MR. MARTIN: I believe that our friends' maid is going crazy . . . she wants to tell us a story, too.

FIRE CHIEF: Who does she think she is? [*He looks at her.*] Oh!

MRS. SMITH: Why are you butting in?

MR. SMITH: This is really uncalled for, Mary . . .

FIRE CHIEF: Oh! But it is she! Incredible!

MR. SMITH: And you?

MARY: Incredible! Here!

MRS. SMITH: What does all this mean?

MR. SMITH: You know each other?

FIRE CHIEF: And how!

[*Mary throws herself on the neck of the Fire Chief.*]

MARY: I'm so glad to see you again . . . at last!

MR. AND MRS. SMITH: Oh!

MR. SMITH: This is too much, here, in our home, in the suburbs of London.

MRS. SMITH: It's not proper! . . .

FIRE CHIEF: It was she who extinguished my first fires.

MARY: I'm your little firehose.

MR. MARTIN: If that is the case . . . dear friends . . . these emotions are understandable, human, honorable . . .

MRS. MARTIN: All that is human is honorable.

MRS. SMITH: Even so, I don't like to see it . . . here among us . . .

MR. SMITH: She's not been properly brought up . . .

FIRE CHIEF: Oh, you have too many prejudices.

MRS. MARTIN: What I think is that a maid, after all—even though it's none of my business—is never anything but a maid . . .

MR. MARTIN: Even if she can sometimes be a rather good detective.

FIRE CHIEF: Let me go.

MARY: Don't be upset! . . . They're not so bad really.

MR. SMITH: Hm . . . hm . . . you two are very touching, but at the same time, a little . . . a little . . .

MR. MARTIN: Yes, that's exactly the word.

MR. SMITH: . . . A little too exhibitionistic . . .

MR. MARTIN: There is a native British modesty—forgive me for attempting, yet again, to define my thought—not understood by foreigners, even by specialists, thanks to which, if I may thus express myself . . . of course, I don't mean to refer to you . . .

MARY: I was going to tell you . . .

MR. SMITH: Don't tell us anything . . .

MARY: Oh yes!

MRS. SMITH: Go, my little Mary, go quietly to the kitchen and read your poems before the mirror . . .

MR. MARTIN: You know, even though I'm not a maid, I also read poems before the mirror.

MRS. MARTIN: This morning when you looked at yourself in the mirror you didn't see yourself.

MR. MARTIN: That's because I wasn't there yet . . .

MARY: All the same, I could, perhaps, recite a little poem for you.

MRS. SMITH: My little Mary, you are frightfully obstinate.

MARY: I'm going to recite a poem, then, is that agreed? It is a poem entitled "The Fire" in honor of the Fire Chief:

The Fire

The polypoids were burning in the wood
A stone caught fire
The castle caught fire
The forest caught fire
The men caught fire
The women caught fire
The birds caught fire
The fish caught fire
The water caught fire
The sky caught fire
The ashes caught fire
The smoke caught fire

The fire caught fire
Everything caught fire
Caught fire, caught fire.

[*She recites the poem while the Smiths are pushing her offstage.*]

MRS. MARTIN: That sent chills up my spine . . .

MR. MARTIN: And yet there's a certain warmth in those lines . . .

FIRE CHIEF: I thought it was marvelous.

MRS. SMITH: All the same . . .

MR. SMITH: You're exaggerating . . .

FIRE CHIEF: Just a minute . . . I admit . . . all this is very subjective . . . but this is my conception of the world. My world. My dream. My ideal . . . And now this reminds me that I must leave. Since you don't have the time here, I must tell you that in exactly three-quarters of an hour and sixteen minutes, I'm having a fire at the other end of the city. Consequently, I must hurry. Even though it will be quite unimportant.

MRS. SMITH: What will it be? A little chimney fire?

FIRE CHIEF: Oh, not even that. A straw fire and a little heartburn.

MR. SMITH: Well, we're sorry to see you go.

MRS. SMITH: You have been very entertaining.

MRS. MARTIN: Thanks to you, we have passed a truly Cartesian quarter of an hour.

FIRE CHIEF [*moving towards the door, then stopping*]: Speaking of that—the bald soprano? [*General silence, embarrassment.*]

MRS. SMITH: She always wears her hair in the same style.

FIRE CHIEF: Ah! Then goodbye, ladies and gentlemen.

MR. MARTIN: Good luck, and a good fire!

FIRE CHIEF: Let's hope so. For everybody.

[*Fire Chief exits. All accompany him to the door and then return to their seats.*]

MRS. MARTIN: I can buy a pocketknife for my brother, but you can't buy Ireland for your grandfather.

MR. SMITH: One walks on his feet, but one heats with electricity or coal.

MR. MARTIN: He who sells an ox today, will have an egg tomorrow.

MRS. SMITH: In real life, one must look out of the window.

MRS. MARTIN: One can sit down on a chair, when the chair doesn't have any.

MR. SMITH: One must always think of everything.

MR. MARTIN: The ceiling is above, the floor is below.

MRS. SMITH: When I say yes, it's only a manner of speaking.

MRS. MARTIN: To each his own.

MR. SMITH: Take a circle, caress it, and it will turn vicious.

MRS. SMITH: A schoolmaster teaches his pupils to read, but the cat suckles her young when they are small.

MRS. MARTIN: Nevertheless, it was the cow that gave us tails.

MR. SMITH: When I'm in the country, I love the solitude and the quiet.

MR. MARTIN: You are not old enough yet for that.

MRS. SMITH: Benjamin Franklin was right; you are more nervous than he.

MRS. MARTIN: What are the seven days of the week?

MR. SMITH: Monday, Tuesday, Wednesday, Thursday, Friday, Saturday, Sunday.*

MR. MARTIN: Edward is a clerck; his sister Nancy is a typist, and his brother William a shop-assistant.*

MRS. SMITH: An odd family!

MRS. MARTIN: I prefer a bird in the bush to a sparrow in a barrow.

MR. SMITH: Rather a steak in a chalet than gristle in a castle.

MR. MARTIN: An Englishman's home is truly his castle.

MRS. SMITH: I don't know enough Spanish to make myself understood.

* In English in the original.—Translator's note.

MRS. MARTIN: I'll give you my mother-in-law's slippers if you'll give me your husband's coffin.

MR. SMITH: I'm looking for a monophysite priest to marry to our maid.

MR. MARTIN: Bread is a staff, whereas bread is also a staff, and an oak springs from an oak every morning at dawn.

MRS. SMITH: My uncle lives in the country, but that's none of the midwife's business.

MR. MARTIN: Paper is for writing, the cat's for the rat. Cheese is for scratching.

MRS. SMITH: The car goes very fast, but the cook beats batter better.

MR. SMITH: Don't be turkeys; rather kiss the conspirator.

MR. MARTIN: Charity begins at home.*

MRS. SMITH: I'm waiting for the aqueduct to come and see me at my windmill.

MR. MARTIN: One can prove that social progress is definitely better with sugar.

MR. SMITH: To hell with polishing!

[*Following this last speech of Mr. Smith's, the others are silent for a moment, stupefied. We sense that there is a certain nervous irritation. The strokes of the clock are more nervous too. The speeches which follow must be said, at first, in a glacial, hostile tone. The hostility and the nervousness increase. At the end of this scene, the four characters must be standing very close to each other, screaming their speeches, raising their fists, ready to throw themselves upon each other.*]

MR. MARTIN: One doesn't polish spectacles with black wax.

MRS. SMITH: Yes, but with money one can buy anything.

MR. MARTIN: I'd rather kill a rabbit than sing in the garden.

MR. SMITH: Cockatoos, cockatoos, cockatoos, cockatoos, cockatoos, cockatoos, cockatoos, cockatoos, cockatoos, cockatoos.

* In English in the original.—Tranlator's note.

MRS. SMITH: Such caca, such caca, such caca, such caca, such caca, such caca, such caca, such caca, such caca.

MR. MARTIN: Such cascades of cacas, such cascades of cacas, such cascades of cacas, such cascades of cacas, such cascades of cacas, such cascades of cacas, such cascades of cacas, such cascades of cacas.

MR. SMITH: Dogs have fleas, dogs have fleas.

MRS. MARTIN: Cactus, coccyx! crocus! cockaded! cockroach!

MRS. SMITH: Incasker, you incask us.

MR. MARTIN: I'd rather lay an egg in a box than go and steal an ox.

MRS. MARTIN [*opening her mouth very wide*]: Ah! oh! ah! oh! Let me gnash my teeth.

MR. SMITH: Crocodile!

MR. MARTIN: Let's go and slap Ulysses.

MR. SMITH: I'm going to live in my cabana among my cacao trees.

MRS. MARTIN: Cacao trees on cacao farms don't bear coconuts, they yield cocoa! Cacao trees on cacao farms don't bear coconuts, they yield cocoa! Cacao trees on cacao farms don't bear coconuts, they yield cocoa.

MRS. SMITH: Mice have lice, lice haven't mice.

MRS. MARTIN: Don't ruche my brooch!

MR. MARTIN: Don't smooch the brooch!

MR. SMITH: Groom the goose, don't goose the groom.

MRS. MARTIN: The goose grooms.

MRS. SMITH: Groom your tooth.

MR. MARTIN: Groom the bridegroom, groom the bridegroom.

MR. SMITH: Seducer seduced!

MRS. MARTIN: Scaramouche!

MRS. SMITH: Sainte-Nitouche!

MR. MARTIN: Go take a douche.

MR. SMITH: I've been goosed.

MRS. MARTIN: Sainte-Nitouche stoops to my cartouche.

MRS. SMITH: "Who'd stoop to blame? . . . and I never choose to stoop."

MR. MARTIN: Robert!

MR. SMITH: Browning!

MRS. MARTIN, MR. SMITH: Rudyard.

MRS. SMITH, MR. MARTIN: Kipling.

MRS. MARTIN, MR. SMITH: Robert Kipling!

MRS. SMITH, MR. MARTIN: Rudyard Browning.*

MRS. MARTIN: Silly gobblegobblers, silly gobblegobblers.

MR. MARTIN: Marietta, spot the pot!

MRS. SMITH: Krishnamurti, Krishnamurti, Krishnamurti!

MR. SMITH: The pope elopes! The pope's got no horoscope. The horoscope's bespoke.

MRS. MARTIN: Bazaar, Balzac, bazooka!

MR. MARTIN: Bizarre, beaux-arts, brassieres!

MR. SMITH: A, e, i, o, u, a, e, i, o, u, a, e, i, o, u, i!

MRS. MARTIN: B, c, d, f, g, l, m, n, p, r, s, t, v, w, x, z!

MR. MARTIN: From sage to stooge, from stage to serge!

MRS. SMITH [*imitating a train*]: Choo, choo, choo, choo, choo, choo, choo, choo, choo, choo, choo!

MR. SMITH: It's!

MRS. MARTIN: Not!

MR. MARTIN: That!

MRS. SMITH: Way!

MR. SMITH: It's!

MRS. MARTIN: O!

MR. MARTIN: Ver!

MRS. SMITH: Here!

[*All together, completely infuriated, screaming in each others' ears. The light is extinguished. In the darkness we hear, in an increasingly rapid rhythm*:]

* Translator's note: in the French text these speeches read as follows:

MME SMITH.—N'y touchez pas, elle est brisée.
M. MARTIN.—Sully!
M. SMITH.—Prudhomme!
MME MARTIN, M. SMITH.—François.
MME SMITH, M. MARTIN.—Coppée.
MME MARTIN, M. SMITH.—Coppée Sully!
MME SMITH, M. MARTIN.—Prudhomme François.

ALL TOGETHER: It's not that way, it's over here, it's not that way, it's over here, it's not that way, it's over here, it's not that way, it's over here!*

[*The words cease abruptly. Again, the lights come on. Mr. and Mrs. Martin are seated like the Smiths at the beginning of the play. The play begins again with the Martins, who say exactly the same lines as the Smiths in the first scene, while the curtain softly falls.*]

* When produced some of the speeches in this last scene were cut or shuffled. Moreover, the final beginning again, if one can call it that, still involved the Smiths, since the author did not have the inspired idea of substituting the Martins for the Smiths until after the hundredth performance.

THE LESSON

•

A Comic Drama

The Characters

THE PROFESSOR, *aged 50 to 60*
THE YOUNG PUPIL, *aged 18*
THE MAID, *aged 45 to 50*

SCENE: *The office of the old professor, which also serves as a dining room. To the left, a door opens onto the apartment stairs; upstage, to the right, another door opens onto a corridor of the apartment. Upstage, a little left of center, a window, not very large, with plain curtains; on the outside sill of the window are ordinary potted plants. The low buildings with red roofs of a small town can be seen in the distance. The sky is grayish-blue. On the right stands a provincial buffet. The table doubles as a desk, it stands at stage center. There are three chairs around the table, and two more stand on each side of the window. Light-colored wallpaper, some shelves with books.*

[*When the curtain rises the stage is empty, and it remains so for a few moments. Then we hear the doorbell ring.*]

VOICE OF THE MAID [*from the corridor*]: Yes. I'm coming.

[*The Maid comes in, after having run down the stairs. She is stout, aged 45 to 50, red-faced, and wears a peasant woman's cap. She rushes in, slamming the door to the right behind her, and dries her hands on her apron as she runs towards the door on the left. Meanwhile we hear the doorbell ring again.*]

MAID: Just a moment, I'm coming.

[*She opens the door. A young Pupil, aged 18, enters. She is wearing a gray student's smock, a small white collar, and carries a student's satchel under her arm.*]

MAID: Good morning, miss.

PUPIL: Good morning, madam. Is the Professor at home?

MAID: Have you come for the lesson?

PUPIL: Yes, I have.

MAID: He's expecting you. Sit down for a moment. I'll tell him you're here.

PUPIL: Thank you.

[*She seats herself near the table, facing the audience; the hall door is to her left; her back is to the other door, through which the Maid hurriedly exits, calling:*]

MAID: Professor, come down please, your pupil is here.

VOICE OF THE PROFESSOR [*rather reedy*]: Thank you. I'm coming . . . in just a moment . . .

[*The Maid exits; the Pupil draws in her legs, holds her satchel on her lap, and waits demurely. She casts a glance or two around the room, at the furniture, at the ceiling too. Then she takes a notebook out of her satchel, leafs through it, and stops to look at a page for a moment as though reviewing a lesson, as though taking a last look at her homework. She seems to be a well-brought-up girl, polite, but lively, gay, dynamic; a fresh smile is on her lips. During the course of the play she progressively loses the lively rhythm of her movement and her carriage, she becomes withdrawn. From gay and smiling she becomes progressively sad and morose; from very lively at the beginning, she becomes more and more fatigued and somnolent. Towards the end of the play her face must clearly express a nervous depression; her way of speaking shows the effects of this, her tongue becomes thick, words come to her memory with difficulty and emerge from her mouth with as much difficulty; she comes to have a manner vaguely paralyzed, the beginning of aphasia. Firm and determined at the beginning, so much so as to appear to be almost aggressive, she becomes more and more passive, until she is almost a mute and inert object, seemingly inanimate in the Professor's hands, to such an extent that when he makes his final gesture, she no longer reacts. Insensible, her reflexes deadened, only her eyes in an expressionless face will show inexpressible astonishment and fear. The transition from one manner to the other must of course be made imperceptibly.*

The Professor enters. He is a little old man with a little white beard. He wears pince-nez, a black skull cap, a long black schoolmaster's coat, trousers and shoes of black, detachable white collar, a black tie. Excessively polite, very timid, his voice deadened by his timidity, very proper, very much the teacher. He rubs his hands together constantly; occasionally a lewd gleam comes into his eyes and is quickly repressed

During the course of the play his timidity will disappear progressively, imperceptibly; and the lewd gleams in his eyes will become a steady devouring flame in the end. From a manner that is inoffensive at the start, the Professor becomes more and more sure of himself, more and more nervous, aggressive, dominating, until he is able to do as he pleases with the Pupil, who has become, in his hands, a pitiful creature. Of course, the voice of the Professor must change too, from thin and reedy, to stronger and stronger, until at the end it is extremely powerful, ringing, sonorous, while the Pupil's voice changes from the very clear and ringing tones that she has at the beginning of the play until it is almost inaudible. In these first scenes the Professor might stammer very slightly.]

PROFESSOR: Good morning, young lady. You . . . I expect that you . . . that you are the new pupil?

PUPIL [*turns quickly with a lively and self-assured manner; she gets up, goes toward the Professor, and gives him her hand*]: Yes, Professor. Good morning, Professor. As you see, I'm on time. I didn't want to be late.

PROFESSOR: That's fine, miss. Thank you, you didn't really need to hurry. I am very sorry to have kept you waiting . . . I was just finishing up . . . well . . . I'm sorry . . . You will excuse me, won't you? . . .

PUPIL: Oh, certainly, Professor. It doesn't matter at all, Professor.

PROFESSOR: Please excuse me . . . Did you have any trouble finding the house?

PUPIL: No . . . Not at all. I just asked the way. Everybody knows you around here.

PROFESSOR: For thirty years I've lived in this town. You've not been here for long? How do you find it?

PUPIL: It's all right. The town is attractive and even agreeable, there's a nice park, a boarding school, a bishop, nice shops and streets . . .

PROFESSOR: That's very true, young lady. And yet, I'd just as soon live somewhere else. In Paris, or at least Bordeaux.

PUPIL: Do you like Bordeaux?

PROFESSOR: I don't know. I've never seen it.

PUPIL: But you know Paris?

PROFESSOR: No, I don't know it either, young lady, but if you'll permit me, can you tell me, Paris is the capital city of . . . miss?

PUPIL [*searching her memory for a moment, then, happily guessing*]: Paris is the capital city of . . . France?

PROFESSOR: Yes, young lady, bravo, that's very good, that's perfect. My congratulations. You have your French geography at your finger tips. You know your chief cities.

PUPIL: Oh! I don't know them all yet, Professor, it's not quite that easy, I have trouble learning them.

PROFESSOR: Oh! it will come . . . you mustn't give up . . . young lady . . . I beg your pardon . . . have patience . . . little by little . . . You will see, it will come in time . . . What a nice day it is today . . . or rather, not so nice . . . Oh! but then yes it is nice. In short, it's not too bad a day, that's the main thing . . . ahem . . . ahem . . . it's not raining and it's not snowing either.

PUPIL: That would be most unusual, for it's summer now.

PROFESSOR: Excuse me, miss, I was just going to say so . . . but as you will learn, one must be ready for anything.

PUPIL: I guess so, Professor.

PROFESSOR: We can't be sure of anything, young lady, in this world.

PUPIL: The snow falls in the winter. Winter is one of the four seasons. The other three are . . . uh . . . spr . . .

PROFESSOR: Yes?

PUPIL: . . . ing, and then summer . . . and . . . uh . . .

PROFESSOR: It begins like "automobile," miss.

PUPIL: Ah, yes, autumn . . .

PROFESSOR: That's right, miss. that's a good answer, that's perfect. I am convinced that you will be a good pupil. You will make real progress. You are intelligent, you seem to me to be well informed, and you've a good memory.

PUPIL: I know my seasons, don't I, Professor?

PROFESSOR: Yes, indeed, miss . . . or almost. But it will come in time. In any case, you're coming along. Soon you'll know all the seasons, even with your eyes closed. Just as I do.

PUPIL: It's hard.

PROFESSOR: Oh, no. All it takes is a little effort, a little good will, miss. You will see. It will come, you may be sure of that.

PUPIL: Oh, I do hope so, Professor. I have a great thirst for knowledge. My parents also want me to get an education.

They want me to specialize. They consider a little general culture, even if it is solid, is no longer enough, in these times.

PROFESSOR: Your parents, miss, are perfectly right. You must go on with your studies. Forgive me for saying so, but it is very necessary. Our contemporary life has become most complex.

PUPIL: And so very complicated too . . . My parents are fairly rich, I'm lucky. They can help me in my work, help me in my very advanced studies.

PROFESSOR: And you wish to qualify for . . . ?

PUPIL: Just as soon as possible, for the first doctor's orals. They're in three weeks' time.

PROFESSOR: You already have your high school diploma, if you'll pardon the question?

PUPIL: Yes, Professor, I have my science diploma and my arts diploma, too.

PROFESSOR: Ah, you're very far advanced, even perhaps too advanced for your age. And which doctorate do you wish to qualify for? In the physical sciences or in moral philosophy?

PUPIL: My parents are very much hoping—if you think it will be possible in such a short time—they very much hope that I can qualify for the total doctorate.

PROFESSOR: The total doctorate? . . . You have great courage, young lady, I congratulate you sincerely. We will try, miss, to do our best. In any case, you already know quite a bit, and at so young an age too.

PUPIL: Oh, Professor.

PROFESSOR: Then, if you'll permit me, pardon me, please, I do think that we ought to get to work. We have scarcely any time to lose.

PUPIL: Oh, but certainly, Professor, I want to. I beg you to.

PROFESSOR: Then, may I ask you to sit down . . . there . . . Will you permit me, miss, that is if you have no objections, to sit down opposite you?

PUPIL: Oh, of course, Professor, please do.

PROFESSOR: Thank you very much, miss. [*They sit down facing each other at the table, their profiles to the audience.*] There we are. Now have you brought your books and notebooks?

PUPIL [*taking notebooks and books out of her satchel*]: Yes, Professor. Certainly, I have brought all that we'll need.

PROFESSOR: Perfect, miss. This is perfect. Now, if this doesn't bore you . . . shall we begin?

PUPIL: Yes, indeed, Professor, I am at your disposal.

PROFESSOR: At my disposal? [*A gleam comes into his eyes and is quickly extinguished; he begins to make a gesture that he suppresses at once.*] Oh, miss, it is I who am at *your* disposal. I am only your humble servant.

PUPIL: Oh, Professor . . .

PROFESSOR: If you will . . . now . . . we . . . we . . . I . . . I will begin by making a brief examination of your knowledge, past and present, so that we may chart our future course . . . Good. How is your perception of plurality?

PUPIL: It's rather vague . . . confused.

PROFESSOR: Good. We shall see.

[*He rubs his hands together. The Maid enters, and this appears to irritate the Professor. She goes to the buffet and looks for something, lingering.*]

PROFESSOR: Now, miss, would you like to do a little arithmetic, that is if you want to . . .

PUPIL: Oh, yes, Professor. Certainly, I ask nothing better.

PROFESSOR: It is rather a new science, a modern science, properly speaking, it is more a method than a science . . . And it is also a therapy. [*To the Maid:*] Have you finished, Marie?

MAID: Yes, Professor, I've found the plate. I'm just going . . .

PROFESSOR: Hurry up then. Please go along to the kitchen, if you will.

MAID: Yes, Professor, I'm going. [*She starts to go out.*] Excuse me, Professor, but take care, I urge you to remain calm.

PROFESSOR: You're being ridiculous, Marie. Now, don't worry.

MAID: That's what you always say.

PROFESSOR: I will not stand for your insinuations. I know perfectly well how to comport myself. I am old enough for that.

MAID: Precisely, Professor. You will do better not to start the young lady on arithmetic. Arithmetic is tiring, exhausting.

PROFESSOR: Not at my age. And anyhow, what business is it of yours? This is my concern. And I know what I'm doing. This is not your department.

MAID: Very well, Professor. But you can't say that I didn't warn you.

PROFESSOR: Marie, I can get along without your advice.

MAID: As you wish, Professor. [*She exits.*]

PROFESSOR: Miss, I hope you'll pardon this absurd interruption . . . Excuse this woman . . . She is always afraid that I'll tire myself. She fusses over my health.

PUPIL: Oh, that's quite all right, Professor. It shows that she's very devoted. She loves you very much. Good servants are rare.

PROFESSOR: She exaggerates. Her fears are stupid. But let's return to our arithmetical knitting.

PUPIL: I'm following you, Professor.

PROFESSOR [*wittily*]: Without leaving your seat!

PUPIL [*appreciating his joke*]: Like you, Professor.

PROFESSOR: Good. Let us arithmetize a little now.

PUPIL: Yes, gladly, Professor.

PROFESSOR: It wouldn't be too tiresome for you to tell me . . .

PUPIL: Not at all, Professor, go on.

PROFESSOR: How much are one and one?

PUPIL: One and one make two.

PROFESSOR [*marveling at the Pupil's knowledge*]: Oh, but that's very good. You appear to me to be well along in your studies. You should easily achieve the total doctorate, miss.

PUPIL: I'm so glad. Especially to have someone like you tell me this.

PROFESSOR: Let's push on: how much are two and one?

PUPIL: Three.

PROFESSOR: Three and one?

PUPIL: Four.

PROFESSOR: Four and one?

PUPIL: Five.

PROFESSOR: Five and one?

PUPIL: Six.

PROFESSOR: Six and one?

PUPIL: Seven.

PROFESSOR: Seven and one?

PUPIL: Eight.

PROFESSOR: Seven and one?

PUPIL: Eight again.

PROFESSOR: Very well answered. Seven and one?

PUPIL: Eight once more.

PROFESSOR: Perfect. Excellent. Seven and one?

PUPIL: Eight again. And sometimes nine.

PROFESSOR: Magnificent. You are magnificent. You are exquisite. I congratulate you warmly, miss. There's scarcely any point in going on. At addition you are a past master. Now, let's look at subtraction. Tell me, if you are not exhausted, how many are four minus three?

PUPIL: Four minus three? . . . Four minus three?

PROFESSOR: Yes. I mean to say: subtract three from four.

PUPIL: That makes . . . seven?

PROFESSOR: I am sorry but I'm obliged to contradict you. Four minus three does not make seven. You are confused: four plus three makes seven, four minus three does not make seven . . . This is not addition anymore, we must subtract now.

PUPIL [*trying to understand*]: Yes . . . yes . . .

PROFESSOR: Four minus three makes . . . How many? . . . How many?

PUPIL: Four?

PROFESSOR: No, miss, that's not it.

PUPIL: Three, then.

PROFESSOR: Not that either, miss . . . Pardon, I'm sorry . . . I ought to say, that's not it . . . excuse me.

PUPIL: Four minus three . . . Four minus three . . . Four minus three? . . . But now doesn't that make ten?

PROFESSOR: Oh, certainly not, miss. It's not a matter of guessing, you've got to think it out. Let's try to deduce it together. Would you like to count?

PUPIL: Yes, Professor. One . . . two . . . uh . . .

PROFESSOR: You know how to count? How far can you count up to?

PUPIL: I can count to . . . to infinity.

PROFESSOR: That's not possible, miss.

PUPIL: Well then, let's say to sixteen.

PROFESSOR: That is enough. One must know one's limits. Count then, if you will, please.

PUPIL: One . . . two . . . and after two, comes three . . . then four . . .

PROFESSOR: Stop there, miss. Which number is larger? Three or four?

PUPIL: Uh . . . three or four? Which is the larger? The larger of three or four? In what sense larger?

PROFESSOR: Some numbers are smaller and others are larger. In the larger numbers there are more units than in the small . . .

PUPIL: Than in the small numbers?

PROFESSOR: Unless the small ones have smaller units. If they are very small, then there might be more units in the small numbers than in the large . . . if it is a question of other units . . .

PUPIL: In that case, the small numbers can be larger than the large numbers?

PROFESSOR: Let's not go into that. That would take us much too far. You must realize simply that more than numbers are involved here . . . there are also magnitudes, totals, there are groups, there are heaps, heaps of such things as plums, trucks, geese, prune pits, etc. To facilitate our work, let's merely suppose that we have only equal numbers, then the bigger numbers will be those that have the most units.

PUPIL: The one that has the most is the biggest? Ah, I understand, Professor, you are identifying quality with quantity.

PROFESSOR: That is too theoretical, miss, too theoretical. You needn't concern yourself with that. Let us take an example and reason from a definite case. Let's leave the general conclusions for later. We have the number four and the number three, and each has always the same number of units. Which number will be larger, the smaller or the larger?

PUPIL: Excuse me, Professor . . . What do you mean by the larger number? Is it the one that is not so small as the other?

PROFESSOR: That's it, miss, perfect. You have understood me very well.

PUPIL: Then, it is four.

PROFESSOR: What is four—larger or smaller than three?

PUPIL: Smaller . . . no, larger.

PROFESSOR: Excellent answer. How many units are there between three and four? . . . Or between four and three, if you prefer?

PUPIL: There aren't any units, Professor, between three and four. Four comes immediately after three; there is nothing at all between three and four!

PROFESSOR: I haven't made myself very well understood. No doubt, it is my fault. I've not been sufficiently clear.

PUPIL: No, Professor, it's my fault.

PROFESSOR: Look here. Here are three matches. And here is another one, that makes four. Now watch carefully—we have four matches. I take one away, now how many are left?

[*We don't see the matches, nor any of the objects that are mentioned. The Professor gets up from the table, writes on the imaginary blackboard with an imaginary piece of chalk, etc.*]

PUPIL: Five. If three and one make four, four and one make five.

PROFESSOR: That's not it. That's not it at all. You always have a tendency to add. But one must be able to subtract too. It's not enough to integrate, you must also disintegrate. That's the way life is. That's philosophy. That's science. That's progress, civilization.

PUPIL: Yes, Professor.

PROFESSOR: Let's return to our matches. I have four of them. You see, there are really four. I take one away, and there remain only . . .

PUPIL: I don't know, Professor.

PROFESSOR: Come now, think. It's not easy, I admit. Nevertheless, you've had enough training to make the intellectual effort required to arrive at an understanding. So?

PUPIL: I can't get it, Professor. I don't know, Professor.

PROFESSOR: Let us take a simpler example. If you had two noses, and I pulled one of them off . . . how many would you have left?

PUPIL: None.

PROFESSOR: What do you mean, none?

PUPIL: Yes, it's because you haven't pulled off any, that's why I have one now. If you had pulled it off, I wouldn't have it anymore.

PROFESSOR: You've not understood my example. Suppose that you have only one ear.

PUPIL: Yes, and then?

PROFESSOR: If I gave you another one, how many would you have then?

PUPIL: Two.

PROFESSOR: Good. And if I gave you still another ear. How many would you have then?

PUPIL: Three ears.

PROFESSOR: Now, I take one away . . . and there remain . . . how many ears?

PUPIL: Two.

PROFESSOR: Good. I take away still another one, how many do you have left?

PUPIL: Two.

PROFESSOR: No. You have two, I take one away, I eat one up, then how many do you have left?

PUPIL: Two.

PROFESSOR: I eat one of them . . . one.

PUPIL: Two.

PROFESSOR: One.

PUPIL: Two.

PROFESSOR: One!

PUPIL: Two!

PROFESSOR: One!!!

PUPIL: Two!!!

PROFESSOR: One!!!

PUPIL: Two!!!

PROFESSOR: One!!!

PUPIL: Two!!!

PROFESSOR: No. No. That's not right. The example is not . . . it's not convincing. Listen to me.

PUPIL: Yes, Professor.

PROFESSOR: You've got . . . you've got . . . you've got . . .

PUPIL: Ten fingers!

PROFESSOR: If you wish. Perfect. Good. You have then ten fingers.

PUPIL: Yes, Professor.

PROFESSOR: How many would you have if you had only five of them?

PUPIL: Ten, Professor.

PROFESSOR: That's not right!

PUPIL: But it is, Professor.

PROFESSOR: I tell you it's not!

PUPIL: You just told me that I had ten . . .

PROFESSOR: I also said, immediately afterwards, that you had five!

PUPIL: I don't have five, I've got ten!

PROFESSOR: Let's try another approach . . . for purposes of subtraction let's limit ourselves to the numbers from one to five . . . Wait now, miss, you'll soon see. I'm going to make you understand.

[*The Professor begins to write on the imaginary blackboard. He moves it closer to the Pupil, who turns around in order to see it.*]

PROFESSOR: Look here, miss . . . [*He pretends to draw a stick on the blackboard and the number 1 below the stick; then two sticks and the number 2 below, then three sticks and the number 3 below, then four sticks with the number four below.*] You see . . .

PUPIL: Yes, Professor.

PROFESSOR: These are sticks, miss, sticks. This is one stick, these are two sticks, and three sticks, then four sticks, then five sticks. One stick, two sticks, three sticks, four and five sticks, these are numbers. When we count the sticks, each stick is a unit, miss . . . What have I just said?

PUPIL: "A unit, miss! What have I just said?"

PROFESSOR: Or a figure! Or a number! One, two, three, four, five, these are the elements of numeration, miss.

PUPIL [*hesitant*]: Yes, Professor. The elements, figures, which are sticks, units and numbers . . .

PROFESSOR: At the same time . . . that's to say, in short—the whole of arithmetic is there.

PUPIL: Yes, Professor. Good, Professor. Thanks, Professor.

PROFESSOR: Now, count, if you will please, using these elements . . . add and subtract . . .

PUPIL [*as though trying to impress them on her memory*]: Sticks are really figures and numbers are units?

PROFESSOR: Hmm . . . so to speak. And then?

PUPIL: One could subtract two units from three units, but can one subtract two twos from three threes? And two figures from four numbers? And three numbers from one unit?

PROFESSOR: No, miss.

PUPIL: Why, Professor?

PROFESSOR: Because, miss.

PUPIL: Because why, Professor? Since one is the same as the other?

PROFESSOR: That's the way it is, miss. It can't be explained. This is only comprehensible through internal mathematical reasoning. Either you have it or you don't.

PUPIL: So much the worse for me.

PROFESSOR: Listen to me, miss, if you don't achieve a profound understanding of these principles, these arithmetical archetypes, you will never be able to perform correctly the functions of a polytechnician. Still less will you be able to teach a course in a polytechnical school . . . or the primary grades. I realize that this is not easy, it is very, very abstract . . . obviously . . . but unless you can comprehend the primary elements, how do you expect to be able to calculate mentally—and this is the least of the things that even an ordinary engineer must be able to do—how much, for example, are three billion seven hundred fifty-five million nine hundred ninety-eight thousand two hundred fifty one, multiplied by five billion one hundred sixty-two million three hundred and three thousand five hundred and eight?

PUPIL [*very quickly*]: That makes nineteen quintillion three hundred ninety quadrillion two trillion eight hundred forty-four billion two hundred nineteen million one hundred sixty-four thousand five hundred and eight . . .

PROFESSOR [*astonished*]: No. I don't think so. That must make nineteen quintillion three hundred ninety quadrillion two trillion eight hundred forty-four billion two hundred nineteen million one hundred sixty-four thousand five hundred and nine . . .

PUPIL: . . . No . . . five hundred and eight . . .

PROFESSOR [*more and more astonished, calculating mentally*]:

Yes . . . you are right . . . the result is indeed . . . [*He mumbles unintelligibly*:] . . . quintillion, quadrillion, trillion, billion, million . . . [*Clearly*:] one hundred sixty-four thousand five hundred and eight . . . [*Stupefied*:] But how did you know that, if you don't know the principles of arithmetical reasoning?

PUPIL: It's easy. Not being able to rely on my reasoning, I've memorized all the products of all possible multiplications.

PROFESSOR: That's pretty good . . . However, permit me to confess to you that that doesn't satisfy me, miss, and I do not congratulate you: in mathematics and in arithmetic especially, the thing that counts—for in arithmetic it is always necessary to count—the thing that counts is, above all, understanding . . . It is by mathematical reasoning, simultaneously inductive and deductive, that you ought to arrive at this result—as well as at any other result. Mathematics is the sworn enemy of memory, which is excellent otherwise, but disastrous, arithmetically speaking! . . . That's why I'm not happy with this . . . this won't do, not at all . . .

PUPIL [*desolated*]: No, Professor.

PROFESSOR: Let's leave it for the moment. Let's go on to another exercise . . .

PUPIL: Yes, Professor.

MAID [*entering*]: Hmm, hmm, Professor . . .

PROFESSOR [*who doesn't hear her*]: It is unfortunate, miss, that you aren't further along in specialized mathematics . . .

MAID [*taking him by the sleeve*]: Professor! Professor!

PROFESSOR: I hear that you will not be able to qualify for the total doctor's orals . . .

PUPIL: Yes, Professor, it's too bad!

PROFESSOR: Unless you . . . [*To the Maid*:] Let me be, Marie . . . Look here, why are you bothering me? Go back to the kitchen! To your pots and pans! Go away! Go away! [*To the Pupil*:] We will try to prepare you at least for the partial doctorate . . .

MAID: Professor! . . . Professor! . . . [*She pulls his sleeve.*]

PROFESSOR [*to the Maid*]: Now leave me alone! Let me be! What's the meaning of this? . . . [*To the Pupil*:] I must therefore teach you, if you really do insist on attempting the partial doctorate . . .

PUPIL: Yes, Professor.

PROFESSOR: . . . The elements of linguistics and of comparative philology . . .

MAID: No, Professor, no! . . . You mustn't do that! . . .

PROFESSOR: Marie, you're going too far!

MAID: Professor, especially not philology, philology leads to calamity . . .

PUPIL [*astonished*]: To calamity? [*Smiling, a little stupidly*:] That's hard to believe.

PROFESSOR [*to the Maid*]: That's enough now! Get out of here!

MAID: All right, Professor, all right. But you can't say that I didn't warn you! Philology leads to calamity!

PROFESSOR: I'm an adult, Marie!

PUPIL: Yes, Professor.

MAID: As you wish.

[*She exits.*]

PROFESSOR: Let's continue, miss.

PUPIL: Yes, Professor.

PROFESSOR: I want you to listen now with the greatest possible attention to a lecture I have prepared . . .

PUPIL: Yes, Professor!

PROFESSOR: . . . Thanks to which, in fifteen minutes' time, you will be able to acquire the fundamental principles of the linguistic and comparative philology of the neo-Spanish languages.

PUPIL: Yes, Professor, oh good!

[*She claps her hands.*]

PROFESSOR [*with authority*]: Quiet! What do you mean by that?

PUPIL: I'm sorry, Professor.

[*Slowly, she replaces her hands on the table.*]

PROFESSOR: Quiet! [*He gets up, walks up and down the room, his hands behind his back; from time to time he stops at stage center or near the Pupil, and underlines his words with a gesture of his hand; he orates, but without being too emotional. The Pupil follows him with her eyes, occasionally with some difficulty, for she has to turn her head far around; once or twice, not more, she turns around completely.*] And now, miss, Spanish is truly the mother tongue which gave birth to all the neo-Spanish languages, of which Spanish, Latin, Italian, our own French, Portuguese, Romanian, Sardinian or Sardanapalian, Spanish and neo-Spanish—and also, in certain of its aspects. Turkish which is otherwise very close to Greek, which is only logical, since it is a fact that Turkey is a neighbor of Greece and Greece is even closer to Turkey than you are to me—this is only one more illustration of the very important linguistic law which states that geography and philology are twin sisters . . . You may take notes, miss.

PUPIL [*in a dull voice*]: Yes, Professor!

PROFESSOR: That which distinguishes the neo-Spanish languages from each other and their idioms from the other linguistic groups, such as the group of languages called Austrian and neo-Austrian or Hapsburgian, as well as the Esperanto, Helvetian, Monacan, Swiss, Andorran, Basque, and jai alai groups, and also the groups of diplomatic and technical languages—that which distinguishes them, I repeat, is their striking resemblance which makes it so hard to distinguish them from each other—I'm speaking of the neo-Spanish languages which one is able to distinguish from each other, however, only thanks to their distinctive characteristics, absolutely indisputable proofs of their extraordinary resemblance, which renders indisputable their common origin, and which, at the same time, differentiates them profoundly—through the continuation of the distinctive traits which I've just cited.

PUPIL: Oooh! Ye-e-e-s-s-s, Professor!

PROFESSOR: But let's not linger over generalities . . .

PUPIL [*regretfully, but won over*]: Oh, Professor . . .

PROFESSOR: This appears to interest you. All the better, all the better.

PUPIL: Oh, yes, Professor . . .

PROFESSOR: Don't worry, miss. We will come back to it later . . . That is if we come back to it at all. Who can say?

PUPIL [*enchanted in spite of everything*]: Oh, yes, Professor.

PROFESSOR: Every tongue—you must know this, miss, and remember it *until the hour of your death* . . .

PUPIL: Oh! yes, Professor, until the hour of my death . . . Yes, Professor . . .

PROFESSOR: . . . And this, too, is a fundamental principle, every tongue is at bottom nothing but language, which necessarily implies that it is composed of sounds, or . . .

PUPIL: Phonemes . . .

PROFESSOR: Just what I was going to say. Don't parade your knowledge. You'd do better to listen.

PUPIL: All right, Professor. Yes, Professor.

PROFESSOR: The sounds, miss, must be seized on the wing as they fly so that they'll not fall on deaf ears. As a result, when you set out to articulate, it is recommended, insofar as possible, that you lift up your neck and chin very high, and rise up on the tips of your toes, you see, this way . . .

PUPIL: Yes, Professor.

PROFESSOR: Keep quiet. Remain seated, don't interrupt me . . . And project the sounds very loudly with all the force of your lungs in conjunction with that of your vocal cords. Like this, look: "Butterfly," "Eureka," "Trafalgar," "Papaya." This way, the sounds become filled with a warm air that is lighter than the surrounding air so that they can fly without danger of falling on deaf ears, which are veritable voids, tombs of sonorities. If you utter several sounds at an accelerated speed, they will automatically cling to each other, constituting thus syllables, words, even sentences, that is to say groupings of various importance, purely irrational assemblages of sounds, denuded of all sense, but for that very reason the more capable of maintaining themselves without danger at a high altitude in the air. By themselves, words charged with significance will fall, weighted down by their meaning, and in the end they always collapse, fall . . .

PUPIL: . . . On deaf ears.

PROFESSOR: That's it, but don't interrupt . . . and into the worst confusion . . . Or else burst like balloons. Therefore, miss . . . [*The Pupil suddenly appears to be unwell.*] What's the matter?

PUPIL: I've got a toothache, Professor.

PROFESSOR: That's not important. We're not going to stop for anything so trivial. Let us go on . . .

PUPIL [*appearing to be in more and more pain*]: Yes, Professor.

PROFESSOR: I draw your attention in passing to the consonants that change their nature in combinations. In this case *f* becomes *v*, *d* becomes *t*, *g* becomes *k*, and vice versa, as in these examples that I will cite for you: "That's all right," "hens and chickens," "Welsh rabbit," "lots of nothing," "not at all." *

PUPIL: I've got a toothache.

PROFESSOR: Let's continue.

PUPIL: Yes.

PROFESSOR: To resume: it takes years and years to learn to pronounce. Thanks to science, we can achieve this in a few minutes. In order to project words, sounds and all the rest, you must realize that it is necessary to pitilessly expel air from the lungs, and make it pass delicately, caressingly, over the vocal cords, which, like harps or leaves in the wind, will suddenly shake, agitate, vibrate, vibrate, vibrate or uvulate, or fricate or jostle against each other, or sibilate, sibilate, placing everything in movement, the uvula, the

* All to be heavily elided.—Translator's note.

tongue, the palate, the teeth . . .

PUPIL: I have a toothache.

PROFESSOR: . . . And the lips . . . Finally the words come out through the nose, the mouth, the ears, the pores, drawing along with them all the organs that we have named, torn up by the roots, in a powerful, majestic flight, which is none other than what is called, improperly, the voice, whether modulated in singing or transformed into a terrible symphonic storm with a whole procession . . . of garlands of all kinds of flowers, of sonorous artifices: labials, dentals, occlusives, palatals, and others, some caressing, some bitter or violent.

PUPIL: Yes, Professor, I've got a toothache.

PROFESSOR: Let's go on, go on. As for the neo-Spanish languages, they are closely related, so closely to each other, that they can be considered as true second cousins. Moreover, they have the same mother: Spanishe, with a mute *e*. That is why it is so difficult to distinguish them from one another. That is why it is so useful to pronounce carefully, and to avoid errors in pronunciation. Pronunciation itself is worth a whole language. A bad pronunciation can get you into trouble. In this connection, permit me, parenthetically, to share a personal experience with you. [*Slight pause. The Professor goes over his memories for a moment; his features mellow, but he recovers at once.*] I was very young, little more than a child. It was during my military service. I had a friend in the regiment, a vicomte, who suffered from a rather serious defect in his pronunciation: he could not pronounce the letter *f*. Instead of *f*, he said *f*. Thus, instead of "Birds of a feather flock together," he said: "Birds of a feather flock together." He pronounced filly instead of filly, Firmin instead of Firmin, French bean instead of French bean, go frig yourself instead of go frig yourself, farrago instead of farrago, fee fi fo fum instead of fee fi fo fum, Philip instead of Philip, fictory instead of fictory, February instead of February, March-April instead of March-April, Gerard de Nerval and not as is correct—Gerard de Nerval, Mirabeau instead of Mirabeau, etc., instead of etc., and thus instead of etc., instead of etc., and thus and so forth. However, he managed to conceal his fault so effectively that, thanks to the hats he wore, no one ever noticed it.

PUPIL: Yes, I've got a toothache.

PROFESSOR [*abruptly changing his tone, his voice hardening*]: Let's go on. We'll first consider the points of similarity in order the better to apprehend, later on, that which distinguishes all these languages from each other. The differences can scarcely be recognized by people who are not aware of them. Thus, all the words of all the languages . . .

PUPIL: Uh, yes? . . . I've got a toothache.

PROFESSOR: Let's continue . . . are always the same, just as all the suffixes, all the prefixes, all the terminations, all the roots . . .

PUPIL: Are the roots of words square?

PROFESSOR: Square or cube. That depends.

PUPIL: I've got a toothache.

PROFESSOR: Let's go on. Thus, to give you an example which is little more than an illustration, take the word "front" . . .

PUPIL: How do you want me to take it?

PROFESSOR: However you wish, so long as you take it, but above all do not interrupt.

PUPIL: I've got a toothache.

PROFESSOR: Let's continue . . . I said: Let's continue. Take now the word "front." Have you taken it?

PUPIL: Yes, yes, I've got it. My teeth, my teeth . . .

PROFESSOR: The word "front" is the root of "frontispiece." It is also to be found in "affronted." "Ispiece" is the suffix, and "af" the prefix. They are so called because they do not change. They don't want to.

PUPIL: I've got a toothache.

PROFESSOR: Let's go on. [*Rapidly*:] These prefixes are of Spanish origin. I hope you noticed that, did you?

PUPIL: Oh, how my tooth aches.

PROFESSOR: Let's continue. You've surely also noticed that they've not changed in French. And now, young lady, nothing has succeeded in changing them in Latin either, nor in Italian, nor in Portuguese, nor in Sardanapalian, nor in Sardanapali, nor in Romanian, nor in neo-Spanish, nor in Spanish, nor even in the Oriental: front, frontispiece, affronted, always the same word, invariably with the same root, the same suffix, the same prefix, in all the languages I have named. And it is always the same for all words.

PUPIL: In all languages, these words mean the same thing? I've got a toothache.

PROFESSOR: Absolutely. Moreover, it's more a notion than a word. In any case, you have always the same signification, the same composition, the same sound structure, not only for this word, but for all conceivable words, in all languages. For one single notion is expressed by one and the same word, and its synonyms, in all countries. Forget about your teeth.

PUPIL: I've got a toothache. Yes, yes, yes.

PROFESSOR: Good, let's go on. I tell you, let's go on . . . How would you say, for example, in French: the roses of my grandmother are as yellow as my grandfather who was Asiatic?

PUPIL: My teeth ache, ache, ache.

PROFESSOR: Let's go on, let's go on, go ahead and answer, anyway.

PUPIL: In French?

PROFESSOR: In French.

PUPIL: Uhh . . . I should say in French: the roses of my grandmother are . . . ?

PROFESSOR: As yellow as my grandfather who was Asiatic . . .

PUPIL: Oh well, one would say, in French, I believe, the roses . . . of my . . . how do you say "grandmother" in French?

PROFESSOR: In French? Grandmother.

PUPIL: The roses of my grandmother are as yellow—in in French, is it "yellow"?

PROFESSOR: Yes, of course!

PUPIL: Are as yellow as my grandfather when he got angry.

PROFESSOR: No . . . who was A . . .

PUPIL: . . . siatic . . . I've got a toothache.

PROFESSOR: That's it.

PUPIL: I've got a tooth . . .

PROFESSOR: Ache . . . so what . . . let's continue! And now translate the same sentence into Spanish, then into neo-Spanish . . .

PUPIL: In Spanish . . . this would be: the roses of my grandmother are as yellow as my grandfather who was Asiatic.

PROFESSOR: No. That's wrong.

PUPIL: And in neo-Spanish: the roses of my grandmother are as yellow as my grandfather who was Asiatic.

PROFESSOR: That's wrong. That's wrong. That's wrong. You have inverted it, you've confused Spanish with neo-Spanish, and neo-Spanish with Spanish . . . Oh . . . no . . . it's the other way around . . .

PUPIL: I've got a toothache. You're getting mixed up.

PROFESSOR: You're the one who is mixing me up. Pay attention and take notes. I will say the sentence to you in Spanish, then in neo-Spanish, and finally, in Latin. You will repeat after me. Pay attention, for the resemblances are great. In fact, they are identical resemblances. Listen, follow carefully . . .

PUPIL: I've got a tooth . . .

PROFESSOR: . . . Ache.

PUPIL: Let us go on . . . Ah! . . .

PROFESSOR: . . . In Spanish: the roses of my grandmother are as yellow as my grandfather who was Asiatic; in Latin: the roses of my grandmother are as yellow as my grandfather who was Asiatic. Do you detect the differences? Translate this into . . . Romanian.

PUPIL: The . . . how do you say "roses" in Romanian?

PROFESSOR: But "roses," what else?

PUPIL: It's not "roses"? Oh, how my tooth aches!

PROFESSOR: Certainly not, certainly not, since "roses" is a translation in Oriental of the French word "roses," in Spanish "roses," do you get it? In Sardanapali, "roses" . . .

PUPIL: Excuse me, Professor, but . . . Oh, my toothache! . . . I don't get the difference.

PROFESSOR: But it's so simple! So simple! It's a matter of having a certain experience, a technical experience and practice in these diverse languages, which are so diverse in spite of the fact that they present wholly identical characteristics. I'm going to try to give you a key . . .

PUPIL: Toothache . . .

PROFESSOR: That which differentiates these languages, is neither the words, which are absolutely the same, nor the structure of the sentence which is everywhere the same, nor the intonation, which does not offer any differences, nor the rhythm of the language . . . that which differentiates them . . . are you listening?

PUPIL: I've got a toothache.

PROFESSOR: Are you listening to me, young lady? Aah! We're going to lose our temper.

PUPIL: You're bothering me, Professor. I've got a toothache.

PROFESSOR: Son of a cocker spaniel! Listen to me!

PUPIL: Oh well . . . yes . . . yes . . . go on . . .

PROFESSOR: That which distinguishes them from each other, on the one hand, and from their mother, Spanishe with its mute *e,* on the other hand . . . is . . .

PUPIL [*grimacing*]: Is what?

PROFESSOR: Is an intangible thing. Something intangible that one is able to perceive only after very long study, with a great deal of trouble and after the broadest experience . . .

PUPIL: Ah?

PROFESSOR: Yes, young lady. I cannot give you any rule. One must have a feeling for it, and well, that's it. But in order to have it, one must study, study, and then study some more.

PUPIL: Toothache.

PROFESSOR: All the same, there are some specific cases where words differ from one language to another . . . but we cannot base our knowledge on these cases, which are, so to speak, exceptional.

PUPIL: Oh, yes? . . . Oh, Professor, I've got a toothache.

PROFESSOR: Don't interrupt! Don't make me lose my temper! I can't answer for what I'll do. I was saying, then . . . Ah, yes, the exceptional cases, the so-called easily distinguished . . . or facilely distinguished . . . or conveniently . . . if you prefer . . . I repeat, if you prefer, for I see that you're not listening to me . . .

PUPIL: I've got a toothache.

PROFESSOR: I say then: in certain expressions in current usage, certain words differ totally from one language to another, so much so that the language employed is, in this case, considerably easier to identify. I'll give you an example: the neo-Spanish expression, famous in Madrid: "My country is the new Spain," becomes in Italian: "My country is . . .

PUPIL: The new Spain.

PROFESSOR: No! "My country is Italy." Tell me now, by simple deduction, how do you say "Italy" in French?

PUPIL: I've got a toothache.

PROFESSOR: But it's so easy: for the word "Italy," in French we have the word "France," which is an exact translation of it. My country is France. And "France" in Oriental: "Orient!" My country is the Orient. And "Orient" in Portuguese: "Portugal!" The Oriental expression: My country is the Orient is translated then in the same fashion into Portuguese: My country is Portugal! And so on . . .

PUPIL: Oh, no more, no more. My teeth . . .

PROFESSOR: Ache! ache! ache! . . . I'm going to pull them out, I will! One more example. The word "capital"—it takes on, according to the language one speaks, a different meaning. That is to say that when a Spaniard says: "I reside in the capital," the word "capital" does not mean at all the same thing that a Portuguese means when he says: "I reside in the capital." All the more so in the case of a Frenchman, a neo-Spaniard, a Romanian, a Latin, a Sardanapali . . . Whenever you hear it, young lady—young lady, I'm saying this for you! Pooh! Whenever you hear the expression: "I reside in the capital," you will immediately and easily know whether this is Spanish or Spanish, neo-Spanish, French, Oriental, Romanian, or Latin, for it is enough to know which metropolis is referred to by the person who pronounces the sentence . . . at the very moment he pronounces it . . . But these are almost the only precise examples that I can give you . . .

PUPIL: Oh dear! My teeth . . .

PROFESSOR: Silence! Or I'll bash in your skull!

PUPIL: Just try to! Skulldugger!

[*The Professor seizes her wrist and twists it.*]

PUPIL: Oww!

PROFESSOR: Keep quiet now! Not a word!

PUPIL [*whimpering*]: Toothache . . .

PROFESSOR: One thing that is the most . . . how shall I say it? . . . the most paradoxical . . . yes . . . that's the word . . . the most paradoxical thing, is that a lot of people who are completely illiterate speak these different languages . . . do you understand? What did I just say?

PUPIL: . . . "Speak these different languages! What did I just say?"

PROFESSOR: You were lucky that time! . . . The common people speak a Spanish full of neo-Spanish words that they are entirely unaware of, all the while believing that they are speaking Latin . . . or they speak Latin, full of Oriental words, all the while believing that they're speaking Romanian . . . or Spanish, full of neo-Spanish, all the while believing that they're speaking Sardanapali, or Spanish . . . Do you understand?

PUPIL: Yes! yes! yes! yes! What more do you want . . . ?

PROFESSOR: No insolence, my pet, or you'll be sorry . . . [*In a rage*:] But the worst of all, young lady, is that certain people, for example, in a Latin that they suppose is Spanish, say: "Both my kidneys are of the same kidney," in addressing themselves to a Frenchman who does not know a word of Spanish, but the latter understands it as if it were his own language. For that matter he thinks it is his own language. And the Frenchman will reply, in French: "Me too, sir, mine are too," and this will be perfectly comprehensible to a Spaniard, who will feel certain that the reply is in pure Spanish and that Spanish is being spoken . . . when, in reality, it was neither Spanish nor French, but Latin in the neo-Spanish dialect . . . Sit still, young lady, don't fidget, stop tapping your feet . . .

PUPIL: I've got a toothache.

PROFESSOR: How do you account for the fact that, in speaking without knowing which language they speak, or even while each of them believes that he is speaking another, the common people understand each other at all?

PUPIL: I wonder.

PROFESSOR: It is simply one of the inexplicable curiosities of the vulgar empiricism of the common people—not to be confused with experience!—a paradox, a non-sense, one of the aberrations of human nature, it is purely and simply instinct—to put it in a nutshell . . . That's what is involved here.

PUPIL: Hah! hah!

PROFESSOR: Instead of staring at the flies while I'm going to all this trouble . . . you would do much better to try to be more attentive . . . it is not I who is going to qualify for the partial doctor's orals . . . I passed mine a long time ago . . . and I've won my total doctorate, too . . . and my supertotal diploma . . . Don't you realize that what I'm saying is for your own good?

PUPIL: Toothache!

PROFESSOR: Ill-mannered . . . It can't go on like this, it won't do, it won't do, it won't do . . .

PUPIL: I'm . . . listening . . . to you . . .

PROFESSOR: Ahah! In order to learn to distinguish all the different languages, as I've told you, there is nothing better than practice . . . Let's take them up in order. I am going to try to teach you all the translations of the word "knife."

PUPIL: Well, all right . . . if you want . . .

PROFESSOR [*calling the Maid*]: Marie! Marie! She's not there . . . Marie! Marie! . . . Marie, where are you? [*He opens the door on the right.*] Marie! . . .

[*He exits. The Pupil remains alone several minutes, staring into space, wearing a stupefied expression.*]

PROFESSOR [*offstage, in a shrill voice*]: Marie! What are you up to? Why don't you come! When I call you, you must come! [*He re-enters, followed by Marie.*] It is I who gives the orders, do you hear? [*He points at the Pupil:*] She doesn't understand anything, that girl. She doesn't understand!

MAID: Don't get into such a state, sir, you know where it'll end! You're going to go too far, you're going to go too far.

PROFESSOR: I'll be able to stop in time.

MAID: That's what you always say. I only wish I could see it.

PUPIL: I've got a toothache.

MAID: You see, it's starting, that's the symptom!

PROFESSOR: What symptom? Explain yourself? What do you mean?

PUPIL [*in a spiritless voice*]: Yes, what do you mean? I've got a toothache.

MAID: The final symptom! The chief symptom!

PROFESSOR: Stupid! stupid! stupid! [*The Maid starts to exit.*] Don't go away like that! I called you to help me find the Spanish, neo-Spanish, Portuguese, French, Oriental, Romanian, Sardanapali, Latin and Spanish knives.

MAID [*severely*]: Don't ask me. [*She exits.*]

PROFESSOR [*makes a gesture as though to protest, then refrains, a little helpless. Suddenly, he remembers*]: Ah! [*He goes quickly to the drawer where he finds a big knife, invisible or real according to the preference of the director. He seizes it and brandishes it happily.*] Here is one, young lady, here is a knife. It's too bad that we only have this one, but we're going to try to make it serve for all the languages, anyway! It will be enough if you will pronounce the word "knife" in all the languages, while looking at the object, very closely, fixedly, and imagining that it is in the language that you are speaking.

PUPIL: I've got a toothache.

PROFESSOR [*almost singing, chanting*]: Now, say "kni," like "kni," "fe," like "fe" . . . And look, look, look at it, watch it . . .

PUPIL: What is this one in? French, Italian or Spanish?

PROFESSOR: That doesn't matter now . . . That's not your concern. Say: "kni."

PUPIL: "Kni."

PROFESSOR: . . . "fe" . . . Look.

[*He brandishes the knife under the Pupil's eyes.*]

PUPIL: "fe" . . .

PROFESSOR: Again . . . Look at it.

PUPIL: Oh, no! My God! I've had enough. And besides, I've got a toothache, my feet hurt me, I've got a headache.

PROFESSOR [*abruptly*]: Knife . . . look . . . knife . . . look . . . knife . . . look . . .

PUPIL: You're giving me an earache, too. Oh, your voice! It's so piercing!

PROFESSOR: Say: knife . . . kni . . . fe . . .

PUPIL: No! My ears hurt, I hurt all over . . .

PROFESSOR: I'm going to tear them off, your ears, that's what I'm going to do to you, and then they won't hurt you anymore, my pet.

PUPIL: Oh . . . you're hurting me, oh, you're hurting me . . .

PROFESSOR: Look, come on, quickly, repeat after me: "kni" . . .

PUPIL: Oh, since you insist . . . knife . . . knife . . . [*In a lucid moment, ironically*:] Is that neo-Spanish . . . ?

PROFESSOR: If you like, yes, it's neo-Spanish, but hurry up . . . we haven't got time . . . And then, what do you mean by that insidious question? What are you up to?

PUPIL [*becoming more and more exhausted, weeping, desperate, at the same time both exasperated and in a trance*]: Ah!

PROFESSOR: Repeat, watch. [*He imitates a cuckoo*:] Knife, knife . . . knife, knife . . . knife, knife . . . knife, knife . . .

PUPIL: Oh, my head . . . aches . . . [*With her hand she caressingly touches the parts of her body as she names them*:] . . . My eyes . . .

PROFESSOR [*like a cuckoo*]: Knife, knife . . . knife, knife . . .

[*They are both standing. The professor still brandishes his invisible knife, nearly beside himself, as he circles around her in a sort of scalp dance, but it is important that this not be exaggerated and that his dance steps be only suggested. The Pupil stands facing the audience, then recoils in the direction of the window, sickly, languid, victimized.*]

PROFESSOR: Repeat, repeat: knife . . . knife . . . knife . . .

PUPIL: I've got a pain . . . my throat, neck . . . oh, my shoulders . . . my breast . . . knife . . .

PROFESSOR: Knife . . . knife . . . knife . . .

PUPIL: My hips . . . knife . . . my thighs . . . kni . . .

PROFESSOR: Pronounce it carefully . . . knife . . . knife . . .

PUPIL: Knife . . . my throat . . .

PROFESSOR: Knife . . . knife . . .

PUPIL: Knife . . . my shoulders . . . my arms, my breast, my hips . . . knife . . . knife . . .

PROFESSOR: That's right . . . Now, you're pronouncing it well . . .

PUPIL: Knife . . . my breast . . . my stomach . . .

PROFESSOR [*changing his voice*]: Pay attention . . . don't break my window . . . the knife kills . . .

PUPIL [*in a weak voice*]: Yes, yes . . . the knife kills?

PROFESSOR [*striking the Pupil with a very spectacular blow of the knife*]: Aaah! That'll teach you!

[*Pupil also cries "Aah!" then falls, flopping in an immodest position onto a chair which, as though by chance, is near the window. The murderer and his victim shout "Aaah!" at the same moment. After the first blow of the knife, the Pupil flops onto the chair, her legs spread wide and hanging over both sides of the chair. The Professor remains standing in front of her, his back to the audience. After the first blow, he strikes her dead with a second slash of the knife, from bottom to top. After that blow a noticeable convulsion shakes his whole body.*]

PROFESSOR [*winded, mumbling*]: Bitch . . . Oh, that's good, that does me good . . . Ah! Ah! I'm exhausted . . . I can scarcely breathe . . . Aah! [*He breathes with difficulty; he falls—fortunately a chair is there; he mops his brow, mumbles some incomprehensible words; his breathing becomes normal. He gets up, looks at the knife in his hand, looks at the young girl, then as though he were waking up, in a panic*:] What have I done! What's going to happen to me now! What's going to happen! Oh! dear! Oh dear, I'm in trouble! Young lady, young lady, get up! [*He is agitated, still holding onto the invisible knife, which he doesn't know what to do with.*] Come now, young lady, the lesson is over . . . you may go . . . you can pay another time . . . Oh! she is dead . . . dea-ead . . . And by my knife . . . She is dea-ead . . . It's terrible. [*He calls the Maid*:] Marie! Marie! My good Marie, come here! Ah! ah! [*The door on the right opens a little and Marie appears.*] No . . . don't come in . . . I made a mistake . . . I don't need you, Marie . . . I don't need you anymore . . . do you understand? . . .

[*Maid enters wearing a stern expression, without saying a word. She sees the corpse.*]

PROFESSOR [*in a voice less and less assured*]: I don't need you, Marie . . .

MAID [*sarcastic*]: Then, you're satisfied with your pupil, she's profited by your lesson?

PROFESSOR [*holding the knife behind his back*]: Yes, the lesson is finished . . . but . . . she . . . she's still there . . . she doesn't want to leave . . .

MAID [*very harshly*]: Is that a fact? . . .

PROFESSOR [*trembling*]: It wasn't I . . . it wasn't I . . . Marie . . . No . . . I assure you . . . it wasn't I, my little Marie . . .

MAID: And who was it? Who was it then? Me?

PROFESSOR: I don't know . . . maybe . . .

MAID: Or the cat?

PROFESSOR: That's possible . . . I don't know . . .

MAID: And today makes it the fortieth time! . . . And every day it's the same thing! Every day! You should be ashamed, at your age . . . and you're going to make yourself sick! You won't have any pupils left. That will serve you right.

PROFESSOR [*irritated*]: It wasn't my fault! She didn't want to learn! She was disobedient! She was a bad pupil! She didn't want to learn!

MAID: Liar! . . .

PROFESSOR [*craftily approaching the Maid, holding the knife behind his back*]: It's none of your business! [*He tries to strike her with a great blow of the knife; the Maid seizes his wrist in mid-gesture and twists it; the Professor lets the knife fall to the floor*]: . . . I'm sorry!

MAID [*gives him two loud, strong slaps; the Professor falls onto the floor, on his prat; he sobs*]: Little murderer! bastard! You're disgusting! You wanted to do that to me? I'm not one of your pupils, not me! [*She pulls him up by the collar, picks up his skullcap and puts it on his head; he's afraid she'll slap him again and holds his arm up to protect his face, like a child.*] Put the knife back where it belongs, go on! [*The Professor goes and puts it back in the drawer of the buffet, then comes back to her.*] Now didn't I warn you, just a little while ago: arithmetic leads to philology, and philology leads to crime . . .

PROFESSOR: You said "to calamity"!

MAID: It's the same thing.

PROFESSOR: I didn't understand you. I thought that "calamity" was a city and that you meant that philology leads to the city of Calamity . . .

MAID: Liar! Old fox! An intellectual like you is not going to make a mistake in the meanings of words. Don't try to pull the wool over my eyes.

PROFESSOR [*sobbing*]: I didn't kill her on purpose!

MAID: Are you sorry at least?

PROFESSOR: Oh, yes, Marie, I swear it to you!

MAID: I can't help feeling sorry for you! Ah! you're a good boy in spite of everything! I'll try to fix this. But don't start it again . . . It could give you a heart attack . . .

PROFESSOR: Yes, Marie! What are we going to do, now?

MAID: We're going to bury her . . . along with the thirty-nine others . . . that will make forty coffins . . . I'll call the undertakers and my lover, Father Auguste . . . I'll order the wreaths . . .

PROFESSOR: Yes, Marie, thank you very much.

MAID: Well, that's that. And perhaps it won't be necessary to call Auguste, since you yourself are something of a priest at times, if one can believe the gossip.

PROFESSOR: In any case, don't spend too much on the wreaths. She didn't pay for her lesson.

MAID: Don't worry . . . The least you can do is cover her up with her smock, she's not decent that way. And then we'll carry her out . . .

PROFESSOR: Yes, Marie, yes. [*He covers up the body.*] There's a chance that we'll get pinched . . . with forty coffins . . . Don't you think . . . people will be surprised . . . Suppose they ask us what's inside them?

MAID: Don't worry so much. We'll say that they're empty. And besides, people won't ask questions, they're used to it.

PROFESSOR: Even so . . .

MAID [*she takes out an armband with an insignia, perhaps the*

Nazi swastika]: Wait, if you're afraid, wear this, then you won't have anything more to be afraid of. [*She puts the armband around his arm.*] . . . That's good politics.

PROFESSOR: Thanks, my little Marie. With this, I won't need to worry . . . You're a good girl, Marie . . . very loyal . . .

MAID: That's enough. Come on, sir. Are you all right?

PROFESSOR: Yes, my little Marie. [*The Maid and the Professor take the body of the young girl, one by the shoulders, the other by the legs, and move towards the door on the right.*] Be careful. We don't want to hurt her.

[*They exit. The stage remains empty for several moments. We hear the doorbell ring at the left.*]

VOICE OF THE MAID: Just a moment, I'm coming!

[*She appears as she was at the beginning of the play, and goes towards the door. The doorbell rings again.*]

MAID [*aside*]: She's certainly in a hurry, this one! [*Aloud*:] Just a moment! [*She goes to the door on the left, and opens it.*] Good morning, miss! You are the new pupil? You have come for the lesson? The Professor is expecting you. I'll go tell him that you've come. He'll be right down. Come in, miss, come in!

June, 1950

JACK
OR
THE SUBMISSION

•

A Naturalistic Comedy

The Characters

JACK
JACQUELINE, *his sister*
FATHER JACK
MOTHER JACK
GRANDFATHER JACK
GRANDMOTHER JACK
ROBERTA I } *These two roles must be*
ROBERTA II } *played by the same actress*
FATHER ROBERT
MOTHER ROBERT

SCENE: *Somber decor, in gray monochrome. A messy room. There is a narrow door, not very high, upstage right. Upstage center, a window with soiled curtains, through which comes a pale, colorless light. On the wall hangs a picture that doesn't represent anything; a dirty, old, worn armchair is at stage center with a bedside table; and there are some indefinite objects, strange yet banal, such as old slippers; in a corner perhaps there is a collapsed sofa; and there are some rickety chairs.*

When the curtain rises we see Jack sprawled on the equally sprawled armchair, wearing a cap, and clothes that are too small for him; he wears a sullen, ill-natured expression. Around him his parents are standing, or perhaps they are seated too. Their clothes are shabby.

The somber decor of the beginning becomes transformed by the lighting during the seduction scene, when it grows greenish, aquatic, towards the end of that scene; then it darkens again at the end of the play.

All of the characters, except Jack, could wear masks.

MOTHER JACK [*weeping*]: My son, my child, after all that we have done for you. After all our sacrifices! Never would I have believed you capable of this. You were my greatest hope . . . You still are, for I cannot believe, no I cannot believe, by Jove, that you will go on being so stubborn! Then, you don't love your parents any more, you don't love your clothes, your sister, your grandparents!!! But remember, my son, remember that I gave you suck at the bottle, I let your diapers dry on you, like your sister too . . . [*To Jacqueline*:] Isn't that right, my daughter?

JACQUELINE: Yes, mom, that's true. Oh, after so many sacrifices, and so much finagling!

MOTHER JACK: You see . . . you see? It was I, my son, who gave you your first spankings, not your father, standing here, who could have done it better than I, for he is stronger, no, it was I, for I loved you too much. And it was I, too, who sent you from table without dessert, who kissed you, cared for you, housebroke you, taught you to progress, to transgress, to roll your *r*'s, who left goodies for you in your socks. I taught you to climb stairs, when there were any, to rub your knees with nettles, when you wanted to be stung. I have been more than a mother to you, I've been a true sweetheart, a husband, a sailor, a buddy, a goose. I've never been deterred by any obstacle, any barricade, from satisfying all your childish whims. Oh, ungrateful son, you do not even remember how I held you on my knees and pulled out your cute little baby teeth, and tore off your toe nails so as to make you bawl like an adorable little calf.

JACQUELINE: Oh! Calves are so sweet! Moo! Moo! Moo!

MOTHER JACK: And to think you won't say a word, stubborn boy! You refuse to listen to a word I say.

JACQUELINE: He's plugged up his ears, he's wearing a disgusting look.

MOTHER JACK: I am a wretched mother. I've brought a mononster into the world; a mononster, that's what you are!

Here is your grandmother, who wants to speak to you. She's tottering. She is octogeneric. Perhaps you'll be swayed by her, by her age, her past, her future.

GRANDMOTHER JACK [*octogeneric voice*]: Listen, listen well to me, I've had experience, there's a lot of it behind me. I, too, like you, had a great-uncle who had three addresses: he gave out the address and telephone number of two of them but never that of the third where he sometimes hid out, for he was in the secret service. [*Jack obstinately remains silent.*] No, I've not been able to convince him. Oh! poor us!

JACQUELINE: And here is your grandfather who would like to speak to you. Alas, he cannot. He is much too old. He is centagenet!

MOTHER JACK [*weeping*]: Like the Plantagenets!

FATHER JACK: He's deaf and dumb. He is tottering.

JACQUELINE: He can only toot.

GRANDFATHER JACK [*in the voice of a centagenet*]: Hum! Hum! Heu! Heu! Hum! [*Hoarse but loud*:]

A char-ar-ming tipster
Sang plain-ain-tive-ly-ie . . .
I'm only eigh-eigh-tee-een
And mor-ore's the pi-i-ty-y.

[*Jack remains obstinately silent.*]

FATHER JACK: It's all useless, he won't budge.

JACQUELINE: My dear brother . . . you're a naughty boyble. In spite of all the immense love I have for you, which swells my heart to the breaking point, I detest you, I exceecrate you. You're making our mamma weep, you're unstringing our father with his big ugly police inspector's mustaches, and his sweet big hairy foot full of horns. As for your grandparents, look at what you've done to them. You've not been well brought up. I'm going to punish you. Never again will I bring over my little playmates so that you can watch them make peepee. I thought you had better manners than that. Comes on, don't make our mamma weep, don't make our papa angry. Don't make grandmother and grandfather blush with shame.

FATHER JACK: You are no son of mine. I disown you. You're not worthy of my ancestors. You resemble your mother and the idiots and imbeciles in her family. This doesn't matter to her for she's only a woman, and what a woman! In short, I needn't elegize her here. I have only this to say to you: impeccably brought up, like an aristocrant, in a family of veritable leeches, of authentic torpedoes, with all the regard due to your rank, to your sex, to the talent that you possess, to the hot blood that can express—if you only wanted it to, all this that your blood itself could but suggest with imperfect words—you, in spite of all this, you show yourself unworthy, at one and the same time of your ancestors, of my ancestors, who disown you for the same reason that I do, and of your descendants who certainly will never see the light of day for they'll prefer to let themselves be killed before they ever come into being. Murderer! Patricide! You have nothing more to envy me for. When I think that I had the unfortunate idea of wishing for a son and not a red poppy! [*To Mother Jack*:] This is all your fault!

MOTHER JACK: Alas! My husband! I believed I was doing the right thing! I'm completely half desperate.

JACQUELINE: Ploor mamma!

FATHER JACK: This boy or this toy that you see there, who has come into the world in order to be our shame, this son or this hun, is another one of your stupid female tricks.

MOTHER JACK: Alack and alas! [*To her son*:] You see, because of you I suffer all this from your father who no longer minces his feelings and now abuses me.

JACQUELINE [*to her brother*]: Go on, tell it to the turkies.

FATHER JACK: Useless to linger longer crying over a destiny irrevocably spilt. I'll remain here no more. I want to remain worthy of my bearfors. The whole tradition, all of it, remains with me. I'm blowing this joint. Frew it!

MOTHER JACK: Oh! Oh! Oh! don't go away. [*To her son*:]

You see, because of you, your father is leaving us.

JACQUELINE [*sighing*]: Kangareen!

GRANDFATHER JACK [*singing*]: A . . . charm . . . ing . . . tip . . . ster . . . sang . . . mur-mur . . . ing.

GRANDMOTHER JACK [*to the old man*]: Be quiet. Be quiet or I'll smack you.

[*She hits him on the head with her fist, and smashes in his cap.*]

FATHER JACK: Once and for all, I'm leaving this room to its own destiny. There's nothing else to do, anyway. I'm going to my bedroom next door. I'll pack my bags and you'll never see me again except at mealtimes and sometimes during the day and in the night to get a bite to eat. [*To Jack*:] And you'll pay me back for your nastiness. And to think it was all to make Jupiter jubilate!

JACQUELINE: Oh, Father, this is the obnubilation of puberty.

FATHER JACK: That's enough! Useless. [*He goes to the door.*] Farewell, Son of a pig in a poke, farewell, Wife, farewell, Brother, farewell, Sister of your brother.

[*He exits with a violently resolute step.*]

JACQUELINE [*bitterly*]: Of a pig in a poke! [*To her brother*:] How can you tolerate that? He's insulting her and insulting himself. And vice versa.

MOTHER JACK [*to her son*]: You see, you see, you are disowned, wretch. He'll will you the whole inheritance, but he can't, thank heaven!

JACQUELINE [*to her brother*]: It's the first time, if not the last, that he has made such a scene with mamma, and I have no idea how we're going to get out of it.

MOTHER JACK: Son! Son! Listen to me. I beg you, do not reply to my brave mother's heart, but speak to me, without reflecting on what you say. It is the best way to think correctly, as an intellectual and as a good son. [*She waits in vain for a reply; Jack obstinately remains silent.*] But you are not a good son. Come, Jacqueline, you alone have sense enough to come in out of the rain.

JACQUELINE: Oh! Mother, all roads lead to Rome.

MOTHER JACK: Let's leave your brother to his slow consumption.

JACQUELINE: Or rather to his consumbrition!

MOTHER JACK [*She starts to go, weeping, pulling her daughter by the hand, who goes unwillingly, turning her head back towards her brother. At the door Mother Jack pronounces this henceforth historic sentence*]: We'll hear about you in the newspapers, actograph!

JACQUELINE: Pawnbroker!

[*They exit together, followed by the Grandfather and the Grandmother, but they go no farther than the embrasure of the door where they remain to spy, visible to the audience.*]

GRANDMOTHER JACK: Keep a watch . . . on his telephone, that's all I can tell you.

GRANDFATHER JACK [*singing waveringly*]:

Fi-i-il-thy but honest . . .
The tip-ip-ster sang . . . [*He exits.*]

JACK [*alone, he remains silent a long moment, absorbed in his thoughts, then gravely*]: Let's pretend that I've said nothing, and anyway, what do they want of me?

[*Silence. At the end of a long moment, Jacqueline re-enters. She goes towards her brother with an air of profound conviction; she goes up to him, stares him straight in the eye, and says*:]

JACQUELINE: Listen to me, my dear brother, dear colleague, and dear compatriot, I am going to speak to you as between the two candid eyes of brother and sister. I come to you one last time, which will certainly not be the last, but what'll you have, so much the worse. You do not understand that I have been sent to you, like a letter through the mails, stamped, stamped, by my aerial voices, bloody bad.

[*Jack remains somber.*]

JACK: Alas, blood will tell!

JACQUELINE [*she's got it*]: Ah, at last! There you've blurted out the key word!

JACK [*desperate, with a most woebegone expression*]: Show me that you are a sister worthy of a brother such as I.

JACQUELINE: Far be it from me to be guilty of such a fault. I'm going to teach you one thing. I'm not an abracante, he's not an abracante, she is not an abracante, nor are you an abracante.

JACK: So?

JACQUELINE: You don't understand me because you don't follow me. It's very simple.

JACK: That's what you think! For sisters like you hours don't count, but what a waste of time!

JACQUELINE: That's not the point. None of that has anything to do with me. But History has her eyes on us.

JACK: Oh words, what crimes are committed in your name!

JACQUELINE: I'm going to tell you the whole thing in twenty-seven words. Here it is, and try to remember it: You are chronometrable.

JACK: And the rest?

JACQUELINE: That's all. The twenty-seven words are contained in those three words, according to their gender.

JACK: Chro-no-me-trable! [*Frightened, an anguished cry*:] But, it's not possible! It's not possible!

[*He gets up, walks feverishly from one end of the stage to the other.*]

JACQUELINE: Oh yes, it is. You've got to figure it out.

JACK: Chronometrable! Chronometrable! Me? [*He calms down little by little, sits down, reflects at length, sprawled out in the armchair.*] This is not possible and if it is possible, it's frightful. But, then, I must. Cruel indecision! There's no legal protection. Hideous, frightful! All law becomes self-destroying when it's not defended.

[*Jacqueline, smiling with a triumphant air, leaves him to his agitation; she exits on tiptoe.*]

MOTHER JACK [*at the door, in a low voice*]: Did the system work?

JACQUELINE [*a finger to her lips*]: Shh! My dear mamma! We

must wait, wait for the result of the operation.

[*They exit. Jack is agitated, he is about to make a decision.*]

JACK: Let's abide by the circumstances, the conclusions oblige me. It's tough, but it's the game of the rule. It applies in such cases. [*Mute debate with his conscience. Occasionally, from time to time, he mutters: "Chro-nome-trable, chr-no-me-trable?" Then, finally, worn out, in a loud voice:*] Oh well, yes, yes, na, I adore hashed brown potatoes!

[*Mother Jack and Jacqueline, who have been spying on him and only waiting for this, enter quickly, exultantly, followed by the Grandparents.*]

MOTHER JACK: Oh, my son, you are truly my son!

JACQUELINE [*to her mother*]: I told you that my idea would get him on his feet again.

GRANDMOTHER JACK: I certainly told you that to make carrots boil you have to . . .

MOTHER JACK [*to her daughter*]: Go on, little vixen. [*She embraces her son, who lets her do so without showing any sign of pleasure.*] My boy! It's really true, you really love hashed brown potatoes? You make me so happy.

JACK [*without conviction*]: Yes, I like them, I adore them!

MOTHER JACK: I'm happy, I'm proud of you! Say it again, my little Jack, say it again, let me hear it.

JACK [*like an automaton*]: I adore hashed brown potatoes! I adore hashed brown potatoes! I adore hashed brown potatoes!

JACQUELINE [*to her mother*]: Oh, you're the clever one! Don't abuse your child if you'd be a truly motherly mother. Oh, that's making Grandfather sing.

GRANDFATHER JACK [*singing*]:

A char-mar-mink tip-ip-ster
was singing a song
melan-cho-li-ly and so-o-omber
full of joy and li-i-ight . . .
Let . . . the . . . little . . . children
amu-mu-se themselves without gi-i-iggling

They'll . . . have plenty of time
to ru . . . ru . . . run
after the girls-girls-irls!

MOTHER JACK [*towards the door*]: Gaston, come here! Your son, your son adores hashed brown potatoes!

JACQUELINE [*same*]: Come, Papa, he's just said that he adores hashed brown potatoes!

FATHER JACK [*entering, severe*]: Is this really true?

MOTHER JACK [*to her son*]: Tell your father, my little Jackie, what you just told your sister, and what you told your darling mother all overcome with motherly feelings that shake her with delight.

JACK: I love hashed brown potatoes!

JACQUELINE: You adore them!

FATHER JACK: What?

MOTHER JACK: Speak, my darling.

JACK: Hashed brown potatoes. I adore hashed brown potatoes.

FATHER JACK [*aside*]: Can it be that all is not lost? That would be too wonderful, but not a moment too soon. [*To his wife and daughter*:] The whole shebang?

JACQUELINE: Oh, yes, Papa, didn't you hear?

MOTHER JACK: Have confidence in your son . . . your son of sons.

GRANDMOTHER JACK: The son of my son is my son . . . and my son is your son. There is no other son.

FATHER JACK [*to his son*]: My son, solemnly, come to my arms. [*He does not embrace him.*] That's enough. I take back my renunciation. I am happy that you adore hashed brown potatoes. I reintegrate you with your ancestors. With tradition. With hashing. With everything. [*To Jacqueline*:] But he must still believe in regional aspirations.

GRANDMOTHER JACK: That's important too!

JACQUELINE: That will come, Papa, have patience, don't worry, Papa!

GRANDFATHER JACK: The char-ar-arming tip-ip-ster!

GRANDMOTHER JACK [*hitting the old man on the head*]: Crap!!!

FATHER JACK: I pardon you then. I overlook, and involuntarily moreover, all your youthful faults as well as mine, and naturally I am going to let you in on the profits of our familial and national endeavors.

MOTHER JACK: How good you are.

JACQUELINE: Oh, indigent Father!

FATHER JACK: Listen. I'm thinking it over. [*To his son*:] You will percuss. So keep at it.

JACK [*in a smothered voice*]: I adore potatoes!

JACQUELINE: Let's not waste time.

MOTHER JACK [*to her husband*]: Gaston, if that's the case, if things are that way, we could marry him off. We were only waiting for him to make honorable amends, and two would have been better than one, and he has done it. Jack, all is under control, the plan foreseen at the beginning is already realized, the engagement is completely prepared, your fiancée is here. And her parents, too. Jack, you may remain seated. Your resigned air satisfies me. But be polished to your fingernails . . .

JACK: Ouf! Yes.

FATHER JACK [*striking his hands together*]: Let the fiancée enter then!

JACK: Oh! That's the agreed-on signal!

[*Enter Roberta, the fiancée, Father Robert, and Mother Robert. Father Robert enters first, big, fat, majestic, then Mother Robert, a round ball, very heavy; then the parents separate in order to let Roberta herself enter, advancing between her father and mother. She is wearing a wedding gown; her white veil conceals her face; her entrance must make a sensation. Mother Jack joyously crosses her hands on her breast; in ecstasy, she lifts her hands to heaven, then goes up to Roberta, looks at her up close, touches her, at first timidly, then paws her vigorously and finally sniffs her. Roberta's parents encourage her with friendly and eager gestures; the Grandmother also must smell the fiancée, and the Grandfather should too, while singing "Too-oo old! . . . Char-ar-mi-ing tip-ip-ipster." Father Jack does the same. Jacqueline, at the entrance of Roberta, gaily claps her hands and shouts out:*]

JACQUELINE: The future is ours!

[*Then, approaching Roberta, she lifts up her dress, screams in her ear, and, finally, smells her. The behavior of Father Jack is more dignified and restrained; he continues to exchange naughty glances and gestures with Father Robert. As for Mother Robert, at the end of the scene she finds herself immobile downstage to the left, a large smug smile on her face. The old Grandfather makes ribald, indecent gestures, wanting to do more but prevented by the old Grandmother, who says:*]

GRANDMOTHER JACK: Come . . . on . . . no . . . but . . . come . . . on . . . you're making me . . . jea . . . lous!

[*While the others are sniffing Roberta, Jack alone seems to be unimpressed; he remains seated, impassive; he snaps out a single word of scorn, aside:*]

JACK: Hill billy!

[*Mother Robert, during this appreciation, appears to be slightly intrigued, but this is only a very fugitive restlessness, and she goes back to smiling again. She makes a sign to Roberta that she should approach Jack, but Roberta is timid, and advances downstage only when led, almost dragged, by Father Robert and pushed by Mother Jack and Jacqueline. Jack makes no movement, his face remains blank.*]

FATHER JACK [*noticing that something isn't right, he remains in the background for a moment, hands on hips, murmuring*]: At least I won't be caught with my pants down.

[*Near to Jack, Father Robert catalogs his daughter, assisted by Jacqueline, Mother Jack, Mother Robert, and the Grandparents.*]

FATHER ROBERT: She's got feet. They're truffled.

[*Jacqueline lifts up the fiancée's dress to convince Jack.*]

JACK [*lightly raising his shoulder*]: That's natural!

JACQUELINE: And they're for walking.

MOTHER JACK: For walking!

GRANDMOTHER JACK: Why yes, the better to twickle you.

MOTHER ROBERT [*to her daughter*]: Let's see, prove it.

[*Roberta walks with her feet.*]

FATHER ROBERT: And she's got a hand!

MOTHER ROBERT: Show it.

[*Roberta shows a hand to Jack, almost sticking her fingers into his eyes.*]

GRANDMOTHER JACK [*nobody listens to her*]: Do you want a piece of advice?

JACQUELINE: For scouring pots and pans . . .

JACK: Sure enough! Sure enough! But I suspected as much.

FATHER ROBERT: And toes.

JACQUELINE: To stub! . . .

MOTHER JACK: But yes, my child!

FATHER ROBERT: And she's got armpits!

JACQUELINE: For turnspits.

GRANDMOTHER JACK [*nobody listens to her*]: Do you want a piece of advice?

MOTHER ROBERT: And what calves! true calves!

GRANDMOTHER JACK: Ah yes, like in my time!

JACK [*uninterested*]: Melanchton did better!

GRANDFATHER JACK [*singing*]: A char . . . ar . . . ming tip-ip . . . ip . . . ster . . .

GRANDMOTHER JACK [*to the old man*]: Come on, make love to me, you're my husband!

FATHER JACK: Listen carefully to me, my son. I hope that you have understood.

JACK [*resigned, acquiescent*]: Oh yes, of course . . . I was forgetting . . .

FATHER ROBERT: She's got hips . . .

MOTHER JACK: All the better to eat you, my child!

FATHER ROBERT: And then she's got green pimples on her beige skin, red breasts on a mauve background, an illuminated navel, a tongue the color of tomato sauce, pan-browned square shoulders, and all the meat needed to merit the highest commendation. What more do you need?

GRANDFATHER JACK [*singing*]: A char . . . ar . . . ming tip . . . ip . . . ster!

JACQUELINE [*shaking her head, lifting her arms, and letting them fall*]: Ah, what a brother I'm stuck with!

MOTHER JACK: He's always been difficult. I had a hard time bringing him up. All he liked was hahaha.

MOTHER ROBERT: But my dear, that's incomprehensible, it's incredible! I'd never have thought that! If I'd known this in time, I'd have taken precautions . . .

FATHER ROBERT [*proud, a little wounded*]: She's our only daughter.

GRANDFATHER JACK [*singing*]: A char . . . ar . . . ming . . . tip . . . ip . . . ster!

MOTHER JACK: This distresses me!

FATHER JACK: Jack, this is my last warning!

GRANDMOTHER JACK: Do you want a piece of advice?

JACK: Good. Then we agree! That'll go with the potatoes.

[*General relief, effervescence, congratulations.*]

JACQUELINE: His honorable sentiments always end up by getting the upper hand. [*She smiles at Jack.*]

FATHER JACK: Now it's my turn to ask a simple question. Don't take it badly.

FATHER ROBERT: Oh no, it's different. Go ahead.

FATHER JACK: One single uncertainty: are there trunks?

GRANDFATHER JACK [*ribaldly*]: Hi . . . hii . . .

MOTHER ROBERT: Ah that . . .

MOTHER JACK: Perhaps that's asking too much.

FATHER ROBERT: I believe . . . heu . . . yes . . . they must be there . . . but I wouldn't know how to tell you . . .

FATHER JACK: And where then?

JACQUELINE: But Papa, don't you see, in the trunks, Papa, really!

FATHER JACK: Perfect. That's perfect. Completely satisfied.

Agreed.

GRANDMOTHER JACK: Would you like a piece of advice?

MOTHER ROBERT: Ah . . . happily!

FATHER ROBERT: I knew that everything would be all right!

GRANDFATHER JACK [*singing*]:

A . . . char . . . arming . . . tipster . . .
In the streets of Paris . . . [*He waltzes.*]

MOTHER JACK: In short, you'll have nothing to fear, the fit's in the fire.

FATHER JACK [*to his son*]: Good! It's a bargain. Your heart has chosen in spite of yourself!

MOTHER JACK: The word "heart" always makes me weep.

MOTHER ROBERT: Me too, it melts me.

FATHER ROBERT: It melts me in one eye, it makes me cry in the other two.

FATHER JACK: That's the truth!

JACQUELINE: Oh, there's no need to be astonished. All parents feel that way. It's a sort of sensitivity, in the true sense of the word.

FATHER JACK: That's our business!

JACQUELINE: Don't be angry, Papa. I said it without thinking. But knowingly.

GRANDMOTHER JACK: Do you want a piece of advice?

FATHER JACK: Oh, my daughter always knows how to arrange things! Besides, that's her specialty.

MOTHER ROBERT: What is her specialty?

MOTHER JACK: She doesn't have one, dear!

FATHER ROBERT: That's very natural.

FATHER JACK: Oh, it's not so natural as all that. But she's passing through a phase. [*Changing his tone:*] Finally, in short. Let's place the fiancés face to face. And let's see the face of the young bride. [*To Father and Mother Robert:*] This is only a simple formality.

FATHER ROBERT: Of course, it's normal, go ahead.

MOTHER ROBERT: We were going to suggest it to you.

GRANDMOTHER JACK [*annoyed*]: Do you want a piece of advice! . . . Well, crap!

JACQUELINE: Come on, then, the face of the bride!

[*Father Robert lifts up the white veil which hides Roberta's face. She is revealed all smiles and with two noses; murmurs of admiration, except from Jack.*]

JACQUELINE: Oh! Ravishing!

MOTHER ROBERT: What do you have to say?

FATHER JACK: Ah, if I were twenty years younger!

GRANDFATHER JACK: And me . . . ah . . . euh . . . and me!

FATHER ROBERT: Ha, ah, twenty years to the day! . . . To the window fastener!

FATHER JACK: As much as possible!

MOTHER JACK: You must be proud of her. You really are lucky. My daughter has only one!

JACQUELINE: Don't get upset, Mamma.

FATHER JACK [*to Jacqueline*]: It's your mother's fault.

MOTHER JACK: Oh, Gaston, you're always nagging.

JACQUELINE: This is not the time, Papa, on such a red-letter day!

FATHER ROBERT [*to Jack*]: You've got nothing to say? Kiss her!

GRANDMOTHER JACK: Ah, my little children . . . Would you like a piece of advice? . . . oh . . . crap!

MOTHER ROBERT: This is going to be charming! Oh, my children!

MOTHER JACK [*to Jack*]: You are happy, aren't you?

FATHER JACK [*to Jack*]: Well, then, you are a man. My expenses will be reimbursed.

MOTHER ROBERT: Come on, my son-in-law.

JACQUELINE: Come on, my brother, my sister.

FATHER ROBERT: You will get along well together, the two of you.

MOTHER JACK [*to Gaston*]: Oh, they are truly made for each other, and all the rest that people say on such occasions!

FATHER ROBERT, MOTHER ROBERT, FATHER AND MOTHER JACK, AND JACQUELINE: Oh! My children!

[*They applaud enthusiastically.*]

GRANDFATHER JACK: A char . . . ar . . . ming . . . tip-ipster!

JACK: No! no! She hasn't got enough! What I want is one with three noses. I tell you: three noses, at least!

[*General stupefaction, consternation.*]

MOTHER JACK: Oh! Isn't he naughty!

JACQUELINE [*she consoles her mother, all the time speaking to her brother*:] Aren't you forgetting all the handkerchiefs she'd need in the winter?

JACK: That's the least of my worries. Moreover, they would be included in the dowry.

[*During this scene, Roberta doesn't understand what's going on. The Grandparents remain outside the action. From time to time, the old man wants to sing; the old lady wants to give her advice. Between times, they dance, vaguely miming the action.*]

FATHER JACK: I'm going to pack my bag! I'm going to pack my bag! [*To his son*:] Your finer feelings are not getting the upper hand! Insensate! Listen carefully to me: truth has only two sides, but it's the third side that's best! You can take my word for it! On the other hand, I expected this.

MOTHER ROBERT: It's annoying . . . it's annoying . . . but not terribly . . . if it's only that, everything can still be arranged!

FATHER ROBERT [*jovial*]: This is nothing, there's nothing wrong, ladies and gentlemen. [*He slaps Jack on the shoulder; Jack still sits stiffly.*] We've foreseen this incident. We have at your disposal a second only daughter. And she, she's completely equipped with three noses.

MOTHER ROBERT: She's trinary. In everything, moreover. And for everything.

MOTHER JACK: Oh! What a relief! . . . The important thing is the children's future . . . Hurrah, do you hear, Jack?

JACQUELINE: Do you hear, sweetheart?

FATHER JACK: Let's try again. But I don't have much faith in it anymore. However, if you insist on it . . .

[*He throws angry looks at his son.*]

MOTHER JACK: Oh, Gaston, don't say that. I'm full of hope. Everything will work out.

FATHER ROBERT: Don't be afraid. You'll see. [*He takes Roberta by the hand, turns her head, and leads her to the door.*] You'll see.

ROBERTA I: Goodbye, everybody. [*She curtsies.*]

[*Father Jack is dissatisfied; Mother Jack is disturbed but hopeful, she looks towards her son; Jacqueline is severe and looks at her brother with a disapproving air. Mother Robert is smiling.*]

MOTHER JACK: How sweet she is, nevertheless!

MOTHER ROBERT: That doesn't matter, I tell you. You're going to see the other one now, and you won't have anything to complain about either.

JACK: One with three noses! At least one with three noses! Anyway, it's not so hard as all that.

JACQUELINE: A lily is not a tiger . . . that says it all.

[*Father Robert re-enters, holding by the hand Roberta II, who is dressed the same—after all the role is being played by the same actress; her face with three noses is revealed.*]

JACQUELINE: Thrilling! Oh, Brother, this time you can't hold out for any more.

MOTHER JACK: Oh, my child! my children! [*To Mother Robert*:] You must be darned proud of her!

MOTHER ROBERT: Somewhat, a lot, quite a bit . . . you bet!

FATHER ROBERT [*approaching Jack, holding his daughter by the hand*]: Now, my friend, you're in luck. To the bottle! Your desire has been specifically gratified. Here she is, here she is, your three-nosed fiancée!

MOTHER ROBERT: Here she is, your three-nosed fiancée.

JACQUELINE: So here she is, here she is then . . .

MOTHER JACK: My darling, you see her, she is yours, your little three-nosed bride, just as you wanted her!

FATHER JACK: What's that? You don't speak? You don't see her then? Here she is, here's the three-nosed girl for your special tastes.

JACK: No, I don't want her. She's not homely enough! She's even passable. There are others that are homelier. I want a much homelier one.

JACQUELINE: Well, now, what do you want!

FATHER ROBERT: This is too much. This is intolerable. It's inadmissible.

MOTHER ROBERT [*to Father Robert*]: You're not going to let people ridicule your daughter, your wife and yourself. Yes, we've been lured into this trap only to be ridiculed!

MOTHER JACK [*sobbing*]: Ah! ah! my God! Jack, Gaston, Jack, wicked son! If I had known I'd have strangled you in your last cradle, yes, with my maternal hands. Or I'd have aborted you! Or not have conceived you! I, I, who was so happy when I was pregnant with you . . . with a boy . . . I showed your photo to everybody, to the neighbors, to the cops! . . . Ah! ah! I am an unfortunate mother . . .

JACQUELINE: Mamma! Mamma!

[*The Grandmother gives her bit of advice, the Grandfather begins a song.*]

FATHER ROBERT: You can't get out of it that way. Ah, this can't go on like this!

MOTHER ROBERT: Don't do anything rash!

FATHER ROBERT: I demand reparations, excuses, explanations, and a total cleansing of this stain on our honor which, however, will never be completely erased! . . . at least concurrently . . .

MOTHER JACK: Ah! ah! ah! That word "concurrently" has always made me groan for it evokes concurrence!

JACQUELINE: Mamma, Mamma, don't task your brain! It isn't worth the bubble!

FATHER JACK: What do you expect me to do! Destiny has willed it. [*To his son*:] There's no word for your attitude; henceforth, you will have no need for respect. Don't count on it anymore!

MOTHER JACK: Ah! ah! ah!

JACQUELINE: Mamma, Mamma, my sweet potato Mamma!

JACK: She's not homely enough!

MOTHER ROBERT: What an insolent boy! [*To Mother Jack*:] It's shameful, madam.

JACQUELINE [*to Mother Robert*]: Leave her be! She's going to be sick.

FATHER ROBERT [*to Jack*]: Well then, my dear fellow, what do you want! My daughter, my daughter's not homely enough?

MOTHER ROBERT [*to Jacqueline*]: I don't give a damn if she is sick, your mammery! So much the butter.

FATHER ROBERT [*to Jack*]: Not homely enough! Not ugly enough! Have you really looked at her, have you eyes?

JACK: But I tell you that I don't find her ugly enough.

FATHER JACK [*to his son*]: You don't even know what you're saying!

MOTHER JACK: Ah! ah! ah!

FATHER ROBERT: Not homely enough. My daughter, my daughter to whom I have given so complicated an education? I can't get over it! It's too much!

JACQUELINE [*to her mother*]: Don't faint just yet! Wait for the end of the scene!

MOTHER ROBERT: We must assert our rights! You must demand reparations!

MOTHER JACK [*to Jacqueline*]: The end of the scream?

JACQUELINE [*to Mother Jack*]: No . . . the scene, of this scene . . .

FATHER JACK: That's all right! It's no one's fault! Nobody's to blame.

MOTHER ROBERT: It's the fault of all of you! You pack of hounds! Low scoundrels! Devils! Huns!

MOTHER JACK: Oh! Oh! Is this going to last much longer?

JACQUELINE: I don't think so.

MOTHER JACK: Oh! Oh! Oh!

JACK: But what do you want me to do, she's not homely enough. That's the way it is and that's all there is to it.

MOTHER ROBERT: He goes on insulting us, this puppy!

FATHER JACK: He doesn't know a thing about women!

FATHER ROBERT [*to Jack*]: There's no point in putting on that photogenic little pose. You're not any smarter than we are.

JACK: She's not ugly! She's not ugly! She wouldn't even sour milk . . . she's almost pretty . . .

MOTHER ROBERT: Have you any milk here so that we can see?

FATHER ROBERT: He doesn't want to, he's bluffing. He knows that milk would sour. This just doesn't suit his convenience, the little prick! It's not going to work that way. I'm going to . . .

[*Intervention of the Grandparents*: *advice, song.*]

MOTHER ROBERT [*to her husband*]: No, I beg of you, Robert-Cornelius, none of that here, no blood between your hands, don't be so assassinous, we'll appeal directly to the law . . . in the palace of justice! . . . with all our plates.

FATHER JACK [*in a terrifying voice*]: I wash my hands of this! [*To Jack*:] I dishonor you forever, just like when you were two years old! [*To everyone*:] And you too, I dishonor you all!

JACK: Good. So much the better. This will be over all the faster.

[*Father Jack moves towards his son. A very charged moment of silence, interrupted by*:]

MOTHER JACK: Oh! Oh! Oh! . . . Poo-poo-poo-poo! [*She faints.*]

JACQUELINE: Mamma! Mamma! [*Again a tense silence.*]

FATHER JACK [*to his son*]: Then you've lied to us. I suspected it. I'm nobody's fool. Do you want me to tell you the truth?

JACK: Yes, for it comes from the mouths of little children.

FATHER JACK [*to his son*]: You've lied to us just now . . .

JACQUELINE [*near her mother*]: Mamma . . . Ma . . .

[*She stops and turns her head, like all the other actors, towards the two Jacks. Mother Jack returns to consciousness in order to hear the grave words which Father Jack utters*:]

FATHER JACK [*to his son*]: . . . When you declared to us, on your honor, that you adored hashed brown potatoes. Yes, you ignobly lied, lied, lied! Like alkali! This was nothing but a mean trick unworthy of the respect that we all have borne you in this house with its noble traditions, since your infancy. The reality is really this: You don't love hashed brown potatoes, you've never loved them. You will never love them!!!

[*Stupefaction, awed horror, silent contemplation. Advice from the Grandmother, song from the Grandfather.*]

JACK: I exceecrate them.

FATHER ROBERT: What cynicism!

JACQUELINE: Alas! So far gone. My big brother!

MOTHER ROBERT: The unnatural son of an unfortunate mother and father!

MOTHER JACK: Ooooooh!

FATHER JACK: Let this serve as a revelation to us.

JACK: Whether this serves you as a revelation or not . . . and if it could serve you as a revelation: so much the better for you. There's nothing I can do about it, I was born like this . . . I've done all that was in my power! [*Pause.*] I am what I am.

MOTHER ROBERT [*whispering*]: What an unfeeling heart! Not a nerve twitches in his face . . .

FATHER ROBERT [*whispering*]: He's an intransigent stranger. Worse than that.

[*The characters, except Jack, look at each other. They also look at Jack, who sits mute in his armchair, then they look again at each other in silence. Jack's last speech has created an atmosphere of restrained horror. Jack is truly a monster. They all move away on tiptoe. Roberta II has not uttered a word during this last scene, but by rather distressed gestures and a discouraged attitude of dejection has shown that she was responding to the development of the action, and now she seems lost. She appears to want to follow her parents. She takes a step towards the exit, but a gesture of her father stops her where she is.*]

FATHER ROBERT [*to his daughter*]: You . . . chin up and do your duty!

MOTHER ROBERT [*melodramatically*]: Remain, unhappy girl, with your lover, since you are his presumed spouse.

[*Roberta II makes a gesture of despair, but she obeys. Father Jack, Mother Jack, Jacqueline, Father Robert, Mother Robert exit on tiptoe, horrified, throwing back occasional glances, stopping often and murmuring*:]

"He doesn't like hashed brown potatoes!"

"No! He doesn't like them!"

"He exceecrates them!"

"Oh, they're two of a kind."

"They're well matched."

"The young people nowadays . . ."

"Better not count on their gratitude."

"They don't like hashed brown potatoes."

[*They exit. The Grandparents exit too, more smiling than ever, strangers to the action. They all stay to spy from behind the door, frequently showing one, two, or three heads at a time. We don't see more than their grotesque heads. Roberta II, timidly, humbly, with some difficulty, decides to go sit down facing Jack, who still wears his cap on his head and remains scowling. Silence.*]

ROBERT II [*attempting to win his interest, then, little by little, to seduce him*]: I am by nature very gay. [*She has a macabre voice.*] You could see it if you wanted to . . . I am eccentric . . . I am the gaiety in sorrow . . . in travail . . . in ruin . . . in desolation . . . Ah! Ah! Ah! . . . bread, peace, liberty, mourning and gaiety . . . [*Sobbing*:] They used to call me the gaiety ready to hand . . . the gay distress . . . [*He remains silent.*] Are you reflecting? Me too, at times. But in a mirror. [*At a given moment, she dares to rise, walk, approach Jack, to touch him, more and more sure of herself.*] I am the gaiety of death in life . . . the joy of living, of dying. [*Jack remains obstinately silent.*] They used to call me also gaiety the elder . . .

JACK: Because of your noses?

ROBERTA II: Oh no. It's because I'm taller than my sister . . . sir,

In all the world there's not another like me.
I'm light, frivolous, I'm very serious.
I'm not so serious, nor very frivolous,
I know all about making hay,
And there are other kinds of work I can do
Less well, as well, or even better
I'm just the tonic for you.
I'm honest, but don't trust me,
With me your life will be a ball.
I can play the piano,
I can arch my back,
I've been properly housebroke.
I've had a solid bringing up . . .

JACK: Let's talk about something else!

ROBERTA II: Ah! I understand you, you're not like the others. You're a superior being. Everything I told you was false, yes. Here is something that will interest you.

JACK: It will interest me if it is the truth.

ROBERTA II: Once, I felt like taking a bath. In the bathtub, which was full almost to the brim, I saw a white guinea-pig who had made himself at home there. He was breathing under water. I leaned over in order to see him close up: I saw his snout quiver a little. He was very still. I wanted to plunge my arm into the water in order to seize him, but I was too afraid that he would bite me. They say that these little animals don't bite, but one can never be sure! He clearly saw me, he was watching me, he was on the alert. He had half-opened a tiny eye, and was looking at me, motionless. He didn't appear to be living, but he was though. I saw him in profile. I wanted to see him full face. He lifted his little head with his very tiny eyes toward me, without moving his body. Since the water was very clear, I was able to see on his forehead two dark spots, chestnut colored, perhaps. When I had a good look at them, I saw that they were swelling gently, two excrescences . . . two very tiny guinea pigs, wet and soft, his little ones that were coming out there . . .

JACK [*coldly*]: This little animal in the water, why it's cancer! Actually it was cancer that you saw in your dream. Exactly that.

ROBERTA II: I know it.

JACK: Oh! listen, I feel I can trust you.

ROBERTA II: Speak then.

JACK: When I was born, I was almost fourteen years old. That's why I was able to understand more easily than most what it was all about. Yes, I understood it quickly. I hadn't wanted to accept the situation. I said as much without mincing words. I refused to accept it. But it wasn't to these people you know, who were here a little while ago, that I said this. It was to the others. Those people you know, they don't understand very well . . . no . . . no . . . but they felt it . . . they assured me that someone would devise a remedy. They promised me some decorations, some derogations, some decors, some new flowers, some new wallpaper, new profundities. What else? I insisted. They swore that they would give me satisfaction. They swore it, reswore it, promised formally, officially, presidentially. Registered . . . I made other criticisms in order finally to declare to them that I preferred to withdraw, do you understand? They replied that they would find it hard to do without me. In short, I stipulated my absolute conditions! The situation would surely change, they said. They would take useful measures. They implored me to hope, they appealed to my understanding, to all my feelings, to my love, to my pity. This couldn't go on for long, not for too long a time, they assured me. As for me personally, I would enjoy the highest regard! . . . In order to coax me, they showed me assorted prairies, assorted mountains, assorted oceans . . .

maritime, naturally . . . one star, two cathedrals chosen from among the most successful. The prairies were not at all bad . . . I fell for it! But everything was fake . . . Ah, they had lied to me. Centuries and centuries have passed! People . . . they all had the word goodness in their mouths, a bloody knife between their teeth . . . Do you understand me? I was patient, patient, patient. Someone would surely come to look for me. I had wanted to protest: there was no longer anyone . . . except those people there that you know, who do not count. They deceived me . . . And how to escape? They've boarded up the doors, the windows with nothing, they've taken away the stairs . . . One can't get out through the attic anymore, there's no way out up there . . . nevertheless, according to what I was told, they've left a few trapdoors all over the place . . . If I should find them . . . I absolutely want to go away. If one can't exit through the attic, there's always the cellar, yes, the cellar. It would be better to go out down there than to be here. Anything is preferable to my present situation. Even a new one.

ROBERTA II: Oh yes, the cellar . . . I know all the trapdoors.

JACK: We can understand each other.

ROBERTA II: Listen, I have some horses, some stallions, some brood mares, I have only those, would you like them?

JACK: Yes, tell me about your horses.

ROBERTA II: In my place, I have a neighbor who's a miller. He had a mare who dropped two sweet little foals. Very sweet, very cute. The bitch also dropped two little puppies, in the stable. The miller is old, his eyesight isn't very good. The miller took the foals to drown them in the pond, in place of the little puppies . . .

JACK: Ah! Ah!

ROBERTA II: When he realized his error, it was too late. He wasn't able to save them.

JACK [*a little amused, he smiles*]: Yes? Hm.

[*As Roberta tells her story, Jack's smile becomes a full laugh, but he's still calm. During the following scene both Roberta and Jack develop—very slowly at first—a declamatory style; the rhythm intensifies progressively, then slows down toward the end.*]

ROBERTA II: No, he wasn't able to save them. But it wasn't really the foals either that he drowned. In fact, when he returned to the stable, the miller saw that the foals were there with their mamma; the little puppies were there too with their mamma, who was barking. But his own child, his baby who had just been born, was no longer beside his mother, the milleress. It was really the baby that he'd thrown into the water. He ran quickly to the pond. The child held out his arms and cried: "Papa, Papa" . . . It was heart-rending. Only his tiny arm could be seen which said: "Papa, Papa! Mamma, Mamma." And then he sank, and that was all. And that was all. He didn't see him again. The miller went mad. Killed his wife. Destroyed everything. Set fire to it. Hung himself.

JACK [*very satisfied with this story*]: What a tragic error. A sublime error!

ROBERTA II: But the foals frolic in the meadow. The little puppies have grown big.

JACK: I love your horses. They're intoxicating. Tell me another about a dog, or a horse.

ROBERTA II: The one who was engulfed in the marsh, buried alive, so that you could hear him leaping, howling, and rolling in his grave before he died?

JACK: That one or another.

ROBERTA II: Would you like the one about a horse of the desert, of a city in the Sahara?

JACK [*interested, as though in spite of himself, and louder and louder*]: The metropolis of the desert! . . .

ROBERTA II: All of bricks, all the houses there are made of bricks, the streets are burning . . . the fire runs through underneath . . . the dry air, the very red dust.

JACK: And the fiery dust.

ROBERTA II: The natives there have been dead for a long

time, their cadavers are dessicating in the houses.

JACK: Behind the closed shutters. Behind the red iron grills.

ROBERTA II: Not a man in the empty streets. Not a beast. Not a bird. Not a blade of grass, not even a withered one. Not a rat, not a fly . . .

JACK: Metropolis of my future!

ROBERTA II: Suddenly, in the distance, a horse whinnies . . . han! han! Approaches, han! han! han! han!

JACK [*suddenly happy*]: Oh yes, that's it, han! han! han!

ROBERTA II: Galloping at full speed, galloping at full speed. . .

JACK: Haan! haan! haan!

ROBERTA II: There he is on the great empty square, there he is . . . He whinnies, runs around, galloping, runs around, galloping . . . runs around, galloping, runs around, galloping.

JACK: Han! han! haan! at full speed, galloping, at full speed, galloping . . . Oh yes, han! han! han! galloping, galloping, galloping as hard as he can.

ROBERTA II: His hooves: click clack click clack, galloping, striking sparks. Click . . . clack . . . clack . . . clack . . . vrr . . .

JACK [*laughing*]: Oh yes, yes, bravo, I know, I know what's going to happen. But quickly . . . quickly . . . go on . . . hurrah . . .

ROBERTA II: He trembles, he's afraid . . . the stallion . . .

JACK: Yes, hurrah . . . He whinnies, he cries with fear, han! . . . Han! . . . He cries out his fear, han! han! let's hurry . . . let's hurry . . .

[*A blazing horse's mane crosses from one end of the stage to the other.*]

ROBERTA II: Oh! he won't escape . . . never fear . . . He turns around and around, gallops in a circle . . .

JACK: Bravo, that's it! I see . . . I see . . . a spark in his mane . . . He shakes his head . . . Ah! ah! ah! it burns him! it hurts him!

ROBERTA II: He's afraid! he gallops. In a circle. He rears! . . .

JACK: His mane is blazing! His beautiful mane . . . He cries, he whinnies. Han! han! The flame flashes up . . . His mane is blazing. His mane is burning. Han! han! burn! burn! han! han!

ROBERTA II: The more he gallops, the more the flame spreads. He is mad, he's terrified, he's in pain, he's sick, he's afraid, he's in pain . . . it flames up, it spreads all over his body! . . .

JACK: Han! han! he leaps. Oh, what flaming leaps, flaming flaming! He cries, he rears up. Stop, stop, Roberta. It's too fast . . . not so fast . . .

ROBERTA II [*aside*]: Oh . . . he called me by my given name . . . He's going to love me!

JACK: He's burning too fast . . . It's going to end! Make the fire last . . .

ROBERTA II: It's the fire that goes so fast—the flames are coming out of his ears and his nostrils, and thick smoke . . .

JACK: He screams with fear, he screams with pain. He leaps so high. He has wings of flame!

ROBERTA II: How beautiful he is, he's turning all pink, like an enormous lampshade. He wants to fly. He stops, he doesn't know what to do . . . His horseshoes smoke and redden. Haan! Through his transparent hide, we see the fire burning inside him. Han! he flames! He's a living torch . . . He's only a handful of cinders . . . He's no more, but we hear still in the distance the echo of his cries reverberating, and weakening . . . like the whinnyings of another horse in the empty streets.

JACK: My throat is parched, this has made me thirsty . . . Water, water. Ah! how he flamed, the stallion . . . how beautiful it was . . . what a flame . . . ah! [*Exhausted.*] I'm thirsty . . .

ROBERTA II: Come on . . . don't be afraid . . . I'm moist . . . My necklace is made of mud, my breasts are dissolving, my pelvis is wet, I've got water in my crevasses, I'm sinking down. My true name is Liza. In my belly, there are pools, swamps . . . I've got a house of clay. I'm always cool . . . There's moss . . . big flies, cockroaches, sowbugs, toads. Under the wet covers they make love . . . they're swollen with happiness! I wrap my arms around you like snakes; with my soft thighs . . . you plunge down and you dissolve . . . in my locks which drizzle, drizzle, rain, rain. My mouth trickles down, my legs trickle, my naked shoulders trickle, my hair trickles, everything trickles down, runs, everything trickles, the sky trickles down, the stars run, trickle down, trickle . . .

JACK [*in ecstasy*]: Cha-a-arming!

ROBERTA II: Make yourself comfortable. Why don't you take off this thing that you're wearing? What is it? Or who is it?

JACK [*still in ecstasy*]: Cha-a-arming!

ROBERTA II: What is this, on your head?

JACK: Guess! It's a kind of cat. I put it on at dawn.

ROBERTA II: Is it a castle?

JACK: I keep it on my head all day. At table, in the parlor, I never take it off. I don't tip it to people.

ROBERTA II: Is it a camel? A capricorn?

JACK: It'll strike with its paws, but it can till the soil.

ROBERTA II: Is it a catapult?

JACK: It weeps sometimes.

ROBERTA II: Is it a catarrh?

JACK: It can live under water.

ROBERTA II: Is it a catfish?

JACK: It can also float on the waves.

ROBERTA II: Is it a catamaran?

JACK: You're warm.

ROBERTA II: Is it a caterpillar?

JACK: Sometimes it likes to hide in the mountain. It's not pretty.

ROBERTA II: Is it a catamount?

JACK: It makes me laugh.

ROBERTA II: Is it a cataclysm, or a catalog?

JACK: It screams, it splits my ears.

ROBERTA II: Is it a caterwaul?

JACK: It loves ornaments.

ROBERTA II: Is it a catacomb?

JACK: No!

ROBERTA II: The cat's got my tongue.

JACK: It's a cap.

ROBERTA II: Oh, take it off. Take it off, Jack. My Jack. With me, you'll be in your element. I have some, I have as many as you want, quantities!

JACK: . . . Of caps?

ROBERTA II: No . . . of cats . . . skinless ones!

JACK: Oh, my cat . . .

[*He takes off his cap, he has green hair.*]

ROBERTA II: Oh, my cat . . .

JACK: My cat, my catawampous.

ROBERTA II: In the cellar of my castle, everything is cat . . .

JACK: Everything is cat.

ROBERTA II: All we need to designate things is one single word: cat. Cats are called cat, food: cat, insects: cat, chairs: cat, you: cat, me: cat, the roof: cat, the number one: cat, number two: cat, three: cat, twenty: cat, thirty: cat, all the adverbs: cat, all the prepositions: cat. It's easier to talk that way . . .

JACK: In order to say: I'm terribly sleepy, let's go to sleep, let's go to sleep . . .

ROBERTA II: Cat, cat, cat, cat.

JACK: In order to say: bring me some cold noodles, some warm lemonade, and no coffee . . .

ROBERTA II: Cat, cat, cat, cat, cat, cat, cat, cat.

JACK: And Jack, and Roberta?

ROBERTA II: Cat, cat.

[*She takes out her hand with nine fingers that she has kept hidden under her gown.*]

JACK: Oh yes! It's easy to talk now . . . In fact it's scarcely worth the bother . . . [*He sees her hand with nine fingers.*] Oh! You've got nine fingers on your left hand? You're rich,

I'll marry you . . .

[*They put their arms around each other very awkwardly. Jack kisses the noses of Roberta II, one after the other, while Father Jack, Mother Jack, Jacqueline, the Grandparents, Father Robert, and Mother Robert enter without saying a word, one after the other, waddling along, in a sort of ridiculous dance, embarrassing, in a vague circle, around Jack and Roberta II who remain at stage center, awkwardly enlaced. Father Robert silently and slowly strikes his hands together. Mother Robert, her arms clasped behind her neck, makes pirouettes, smiling stupidly. Mother Jack, with an expressionless face, shakes her shoulders in a grotesque fashion. Father Jack pulls up his pants and walks on his heels. Jacqueline nods her head, then they continue to dance, squatting down, while Jack and Roberta II squat down too, and remain motionless. The Grandparents turn around, idiotically, looking at each other, and smiling; then they squat down in their turn. All this must produce in the audience a feeling of embarrassment, awkwardness, and shame. The darkness increases. On stage, the actors utter vague miaows while turning around, bizarre moans, croakings. The darkness increases. We can still see the Jacks and Roberts crawling on the stage. We hear their animal noises, then we don't see them any more. We hear only their moans, their sighs, then all fades away, all is extinguished. Again, a gray light comes on. All the characters have disappeared, except Roberta, who is lying down, or rather squatting down, buried beneath her gown. We see only her pale face, with its three noses quivering, and her nine fingers moving like snakes.*]

Summer, 1950

THE CHAIRS

•

A Tragic Farce

The Characters

OLD MAN, *aged 95*
OLD WOMAN, *aged 94*
THE ORATOR, *aged 45 to 50*
And many other characters

SCENE: *Circular walls with a recess upstage center. A large, very sparsely furnished room. To the right, going upstage from the proscenium, three doors. Then a window with a stool in front of it; then another door. In the center of the back wall of the recess, a large double door, and two other doors facing each other and bracketing the main door: these last two doors, or at least one of them, are almost hidden from the audience. To the left, going upstage from the proscenium, there are three doors, a window with a stool in front of it, opposite the window on the right, then a blackboard and a dais. See the plan below. Downstage are two chairs, side by side. A gas lamp hangs from the ceiling.*

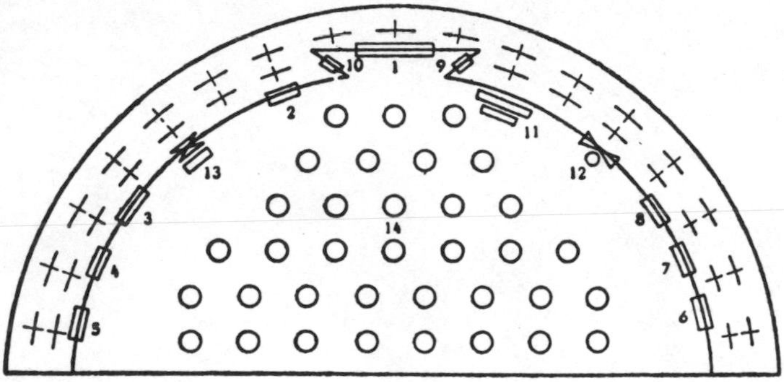

1: Main double door.
2, 3, 4, 5: Side doors on the right.
6, 7, 8: Side doors on the left.
9, 10: Two doors hidden in the recess.
11: Dais and blackboard.
12, 13: Windows, with stools, left and right.
14: Empty chairs.
XXX Corridor, in wings.

[*The curtain rises. Half-light. The Old man is up on the stool, leaning out the window on the left. The Old Woman lights the gas lamp. Green light. She goes over to the Old Man and takes him by the sleeve.*]

OLD WOMAN: Come my darling, close the window. There's a bad smell from that stagnant water, and besides the mosquitoes are coming in.

OLD MAN: Leave me alone!

OLD WOMAN: Come, come, my darling, come sit down. You shouldn't lean out, you might fall into the water. You know what happened to François I. You must be careful.

OLD MAN: Still more examples from history! Sweetheart, I'm tired of French history. I want to see—the boats on the water making blots in the sunlight.

OLD WOMAN: You can't see them, there's no sunlight, it's nighttime, my darling.

OLD MAN: There are still shadows. [*He leans out very far.*]

OLD WOMAN [*pulling him in with all her strength*]: Oh! . . . you're frightening me, my darling . . . come sit down, you won't be able to see them come, anyway. There's no use trying. It's dark . . .

[*The Old Man reluctantly lets himself be pulled in.*]

OLD MAN: I wanted to see—you know how much I love to see the water.

OLD WOMAN: How can you, my darling? . . . It makes me dizzy. Ah! this house, this island, I can't get used to it. Water all around us . . . water under the windows, stretching as far as the horizon.

[*The Old Woman drags the Old Man down and they move towards the two chairs downstage; the Old Man seats himself quite naturally on the lap of the Old Woman.*]

OLD MAN: It's six o'clock in the evening . . . it is dark already. It wasn't like this before. Surely you remember, there was still daylight at nine o'clock in the evening, at ten o'clock, at midnight.

OLD WOMAN: Come to think of it, that's very true. What a remarkable memory you have!

OLD MAN: Things have certainly changed.

OLD WOMAN: Why is that, do you think?

OLD MAN: I don't know, Semiramis, sweetheart . . . Perhaps it's because the further one goes, the deeper one sinks. It's because the earth keeps turning around, around, around, around . . .

OLD WOMAN: Around, around, my little pet. [*Silence.*] Ah! yes, you've certainly a fine intellect. You are very gifted, my darling. You could have been head president, head king, or even head doctor, or head general, if you had wanted to, if only you'd had a little ambition in life . . .

OLD MAN: What good would that have done us? We'd not have lived any better . . . and besides, we have a position here. I am a general, in any case, of the house, since I am the general factotum.

OLD WOMAN [*caressing the Old Man as one caresses a child*]: My darling, my pet.

OLD MAN: I'm very bored.

OLD WOMAN: You were more cheerful when you were looking at the water . . . Let's amuse ourselves by making believe, the way you did the other evening.

OLD MAN: Make believe yourself, it's your turn.

OLD WOMAN: It's your turn.

OLD MAN: Your turn.

OLD WOMAN: Your turn

OLD MAN: Your turn.

OLD WOMAN: Your turn.

OLD MAN: Drink your tea, Semiramis.

[*Of course there is no tea.*]

OLD WOMAN: Come on now, imitate the month of February.

OLD MAN: I don't like the months of the year.

OLD WOMAN: Those are the only ones we have, up till now. Come on, just to please me . . .

OLD MAN: All right, here's the month of February. [*He*

scratches his head like Stan Laurel.]

OLD WOMAN [*laughing, applauding*]: That's just right. Thank you, thank you, you're as cute as can be, my darling. [*She hugs him.*] Oh, you are so gifted, you could have been at least a head general, if you had wanted to . . .

OLD MAN: I am a general, general factotum. [*Silence.*]

OLD WOMAN: Tell me the story, you know *the* story: "Then at last we arrived . . ."

OLD MAN: Again? . . . I'm sick of it . . . "Then at last we arrived"? That again . . . you always ask for the same thing! . . . "Then at last we arrived . . ." But it's monotonous . . . For all of the seventy-five years that we've been married, every single evening, absolutely every blessed evening, you've made me tell the same story, you've made me imitate the same people, the same months . . . always the same . . . let's talk about something else . . .

OLD WOMAN: My darling, I'm not tired of it . . . it's your life, it fascinates me.

OLD MAN: You know it by heart.

OLD WOMAN: It's as if suddenly I'd forgotten everything . . . it's as though my mind were a clean slate every evening . . . Yes, my darling, I do it on purpose, I take a dose of salts . . . I become new again, for you, my darling, every evening . . . Come on, begin again, please.

OLD MAN: Well, if you want me to.

OLD WOMAN: Come on then, tell your story . . . It's also mine; what is yours is mine! Then at last we arrived . . .

OLD MAN: Then at last we arrived . . . my sweetheart . . .

OLD WOMAN: Then at last we arrived . . . my darling . . .

OLD MAN: Then at last we arrived at a big fence. We were soaked through, frozen to the bone, for hours, for days, for nights, for weeks . . .

OLD WOMAN: For months . . .

OLD MAN: . . . In the rain . . . Our ears, our feet, our knees, our noses, our teeth were chattering . . . that was eighty years ago . . . They wouldn't let us in . . . they might at least have opened the gate of the garden . . . [*Silence.*]

OLD WOMAN: In the garden the grass was wet.

OLD MAN: There was a path which led to a little square and in the center, a village church . . . Where was this village? Do you recall?

OLD WOMAN: No, my darling, I've forgotten.

OLD MAN: How did we reach it? Where is the road? This place was called Paris, I think . . .

OLD WOMAN: Paris never existed, my little one.

OLD MAN: That city must have existed because it collapsed . . . It was the city of light, but it has been extinguished, extinguished, for four hundred thousand years . . . Nothing remains of it today, except a song.

OLD WOMAN: A real song? That's odd. What song?

OLD MAN: A lullaby, an allegory: "Paris will always be Paris."

OLD WOMAN: And the way to it was through the garden? Was it far?

OLD MAN [*dreaming, lost*]: The song? . . . the rain? . . .

OLD WOMAN: You are very gifted. If you had had a little ambition in life you could have been head king, head journalist, head comedian, head general . . . All that's gone down the drain, alas . . . down the old black drain . . . down the old drain, I tell you. [*Silence.*]

OLD MAN: Then at last we arrived . . .

OLD WOMAN: Ah! yes, go on . . . tell me . . .

OLD MAN [*while the Old Woman begins to laugh softly, senilely, then progressively in great bursts, the Old Man laughs, too, as he continues*]: Then at last we arrived, we laughed till we cried, the story was so idiotic . . . the idiot arrived full speed, bare-bellied, the idiot was pot-bellied . . . he arrived with a trunk chock full of rice; the rice spilled out on the ground . . . the idiot on the ground too, belly to ground . . . then at last we laughed, we laughed, we laughed, the idiotic belly, bare with rice on the ground, the trunk, the story of sick from rice belly to ground, bare-bellied, all with rice, at last we laughed, the idiot at last arrived all bare, we laughed . . .

OLD WOMAN [*laughing*]: At last we laughed like idiots, at last arrived all bare, we laughed, the trunk, the trunk full of rice, the rice on the belly, on the ground . . .

OLD MAN AND OLD WOMAN [*laughing together*]: At last we laughed. Ah! . . . laughed . . . arrived . . . arrived . . . Ah! . . . Ah! . . . rived . . . arrived . . . arrived . . . the idiotic bare belly . . . arrived with the rice . . . arrived with the rice . . . [*This is all we hear.*] At last we . . . bare-bellied . . . arrived . . . the trunk . . . [*Then the Old Man and Old Woman calm down little by little.*] We lau . . . Ah! . . . aughed . . . Ah! . . . arrived . . . Ah! . . . arrived . . . aughed . . . aughed.

OLD WOMAN: So that's the way it was, your wonderful Paris.

OLD MAN: Who could put it better?

OLD WOMAN: Oh! my darling, you are so really fine. Oh! so really, you know, so really, so really, you could have been anything in life, a lot more than general factotum.

OLD MAN: Let's be modest . . . we should be content with the little . . .

OLD WOMAN: Perhaps you've spoiled your career?

OLD MAN [*weeping suddenly*]: I've spoiled it? I've spilled it? Ah! where are you, Mamma, Mamma, where are you, Mamma? . . . hi, hi, hi, I'm an orphan. [*He moans.*] . . . an orphan, dworfan.

OLD WOMAN: Here I am, what are you afraid of?

OLD MAN: No, Semiramis, my sweetheart, you're not my mamma . . . orphan, dworfan, who will protect me?

OLD WOMAN: But I'm here, my darling!

OLD MAN: It's not the same thing . . . I want my mamma, na, you, you're not my mamma, you . . .

OLD WOMAN [*caressing him*]: You're breaking my heart, don't cry, my little one.

OLD MAN: Hi, hi, let me go, hi, hi, I'm all spoiled, I'm wet all over, my career is spilled, it's spoiled.

OLD WOMAN: Calm down.

OLD MAN [*sobbing his mouth wide open like a baby*]: I'm an orphan . . . dworfan.

OLD WOMAN [*trying to console him by cajoling him*]: My orphan, my darling, you're breaking my heart, my orphan.

[*She rocks the Old Man who is sitting on her knees again.*]

OLD MAN [*sobbing*]: Hi, hi, hi! My mamma! Where is my mamma? I don't have a mamma anymore.

OLD WOMAN: I am your wife, I'm the one who is your mamma now.

OLD MAN [*giving in a little*]: That's not true, I'm an orphan, hi, hi.

OLD WOMAN [*still rocking him*]: My pet, my orphan, dworfan, worfan, morphan, orphan.

OLD MAN [*still sulky, but giving in more and more*]: No . . . I don't wan't; I don't wa-a-a-ant.

OLD WOMAN [*crooning*]: Orphan-ly, orhpan-lay, orphan-lo, orphan-loo.

OLD MAN: No-o-o . . . No-o-o.

OLD WOMAN [*same business*]: Li lon lala, li lon la lay, orphan-ly, orphan-lay, relee-relay, orphan-li-relee-rela . . .

OLD MAN: Hi, hi, hi, hi. [*He sniffles, calming down little by little.*] Where is she? My mamma.

OLD WOMAN: In heavenly paradise . . . she hears you, she sees you, among the flowers; don't cry anymore, you will only make me weep!

OLD MAN: That's not even true-ue . . . she can't see me . . . she can't hear me. I'm an orphan, on earth, you're not my mamma . . .

OLD WOMAN [*he is almost calm*]: Now, come on, calm down, don't get so upset . . . you have great qualities, my little general . . . dry your tears; the guests are sure to come this evening and they mustn't see you this way . . . all is not lost, all is not spoiled, you'll tell them everything, you will explain, you have a message . . . you always say you are going to deliver it . . . you must live, you have to struggle for your message . . .

OLD MAN: I have a message, that's God's truth, I struggle, a mission, I have something to say, a message to communicate to humanity, to mankind . . .

OLD WOMAN: To mankind, my darling, your message! . . .

OLD MAN: That's true, yes, it's true . . .

OLD WOMAN [*she wipes the Old Man's nose, dries his tears*]: That's it . . . you're a man, a soldier, a general factotum . . .

OLD MAN [*he gets off the Old Woman's lap and walks with short, agitated steps*]: I'm not like other people, I have an ideal in life. I am perhaps gifted, as you say, I have some talent, but things aren't easy for me. I've served well in my capacity as general factotum, I've always been in command of the situation, honorably, that should be enough . . .

OLD WOMAN: Not for you, you're not like other people, you are much greater, and moreover you'd have done much better if you had got along with other people, like other people do. You've quarreled with all your friends, with all the directors, with all the generals, with your own brother.

OLD MAN: It's not my fault, Semiramis, you know very well what he said.

OLD WOMAN: What did he say?

OLD MAN: He said: "My friends, I've got a flea. I'm going to pay you a visit in the hope of leaving my flea with you."

OLD WOMAN: People say things like that, my dear. You shouldn't have paid any attention to it. But with Carel, why were you so angry with him. Was it his fault too?

OLD MAN: You're going to make me angry, you're going to make me angry. Na. Of course it was his fault. He came one evening, he said: "I know just the word that fits you. I'm not going to say it, I'll just think it." And he laughed like a fool.

OLD WOMAN: But he had a warm heart, my darling. In this life, you've got to be less sensitive.

OLD MAN: I don't care for jokes like that.

OLD WOMAN: You could have been head admiral, head cabinet-maker, head orchestra conductor.

[*Long silence. They remain immobile for a time, completely rigid on their chairs.*]

OLD MAN [*as in a dream*]: At the end of the garden there was . . . there was . . . there was . . . there was . . . was what, my dear?

OLD WOMAN: The city of Paris!

OLD MAN: At the end, at the end of the end of the city of Paris, there was, there was, was what?

OLD WOMAN: My darling, was what, my darling, was who?

OLD MAN: The place and the weather were beautiful . . .

OLD WOMAN: The weather was so beautiful, are you sure?

OLD MAN: I don't recall the place . . .

OLD WOMAN: Don't tax your mind then . . .

OLD MAN: It's too far away, I can no longer . . . recall it . . . where was this?

OLD WOMAN: But what?

OLD MAN: What I . . . what I . . . where was this? And who?

OLD WOMAN: No matter where it is—I will follow you anywhere, I'll follow you, my darling.

OLD MAN: Ah! I have so much difficulty expressing myself . . . but I must tell it all.

OLD WOMAN: It's a sacred duty. You've no right to keep your message from the world. You must reveal it to mankind, they're waiting for it . . . the universe waits only for you.

OLD MAN: Yes, yes, I will speak.

OLD WOMAN: Have you really decided? You must.

OLD MAN: Drink your tea.

OLD WOMAN: You could have been head orator, if you'd had more will power in life . . . I'm proud, I'm happy that you have at last decided to speak to every country, to Europe, to every continent!

OLD MAN: Unfortunately, I have so much difficulty expressing myself, it isn't easy for me.

OLD WOMAN: It's easy once you begin, like life and death . . . it's enough to have your mind made up. It's in speaking that ideas come to us, words, and then we, in our own words, we find perhaps everything, the city too, the garden, and then we are orphans no longer.

OLD MAN: It's not I who's going to speak, I've hired a professional orator, he'll speak in my name, you'll see.

OLD WOMAN: Then, it really is for this evening? And have you invited everyone, all the characters, all the property owners, and all the intellectuals?

OLD MAN: Yes, all the owners and all the intellectuals. [*Silence.*]

OLD WOMAN: The janitors? the bishops? the chemists? the tinsmiths? the violinists? the delegates? the presidents? the police? the merchants? the buildings? the pen holders? the chromosomes?

OLD MAN: Yes, yes, and the post-office employees, the innkeepers, and the artists, everybody who is a little intellectual, a little proprietary!

OLD WOMAN: And the bankers?

OLD MAN: Yes, invited.

OLD WOMAN: The proletarians? the functionaries? the militaries? the revolutionaries? the reactionaries? the alienists and their alienated?

OLD MAN: Of course, all of them, all of them, all of them, since actually everyone is either inellectual or proprietary.

OLD WOMAN: Don't get upset, my darling, I don't mean to annoy you, you are so very absent-minded, like all great geniuses. This meeting is important, they must all be here this evening. Can you count on them? Have they promised?

OLD MAN: Drink your tea, Semiramis. [*Silence.*]

OLD WOMAN: The papacy, the papayas, and the papers?

OLD MAN: I've invited them. [*Silence.*] I'm going to communicate the message to them . . . All my life, I've felt that I was suffocating; and now, they will know all, thanks to you and to the Orator, you are the only ones who have understood me.

OLD WOMAN: I'm so proud of you . . .

OLD MAN: The meeting will take place in a few minutes.

OLD WOMAN: It's true then, they're going to come, this evening? You won't feel like crying any more, the intellectuals and the proprietors will take the place of papas and mammas? [*Silence.*] Couldn't you put off this meeting? It won't be too tiring for us?

[*More violent agitation. For several moments the Old Man has been turning around the Old Woman with the short, hesitant steps of an old man or of a child. He takes a step or two towards one of the doors, then returns and walks around her again.*]

OLD MAN: You really think this might tire us?

OLD WOMAN: You have a slight cold.

OLD MAN: How can I call it off?

OLD WOMAN: Invite them for another evening. You could telephone.

OLD MAN: No, my God, I can't do that, it's too late. They've probably already embarked!

OLD WOMAN: You should have been more careful.

[*We hear the sound of a boat gliding through the water.*]

OLD MAN: I think someone is coming already . . . [*The gliding sound of a boat is heard more clearly.*] . . . Yes, they're coming! . . .

[*The Old Woman gets up also and walks with a hobble.*]

OLD WOMAN: Perhaps it's the Orator.

OLD MAN: He won't come so soon. This must be somebody else. [*We hear the doorbell ring.*] Ah!

OLD WOMAN: Ah!

[*Nervously, the Old Man and the Old Woman move towards the concealed door in the recess to the right. As they move upstage, they say:*]

OLD MAN: Come on . . .

OLD WOMAN: My hair must look a sight . . . wait a moment . . .

[*She arranges her hair and her dress as she hobbles along, pulling up her thick red stockings.*]

OLD MAN: You should have gotten ready before . . . you had

plenty of time.

OLD WOMAN: I'm so badly dressed . . . I'm wearing an old gown and it's all rumpled . . .

OLD MAN: All you had to do was to press it . . . hurry up! You're making our guests wait.

[*The Old Man, followed by the Old woman still grumbling, reaches the door in the recess; we don't see them for a moment; we hear them open the door, then close it again after having shown someone in.*]

VOICE OF OLD MAN: Good evening, madam, won't you please come in. We're delighted to see you. This is my wife.

VOICE OF OLD WOMAN: Good evening, madam, I am very happy to make your acquaintance. Take care, don't ruin your hat. You might take out the hatpin, that will be more comfortable. Oh! no, no one will sit on it.

VOICE OF OLD MAN: Put your fur down there. Let me help you. No, nothing will happen to it.

VOICE OF OLD WOMAN: Oh! what a pretty suit . . . and such darling colors in your blouse . . . Won't you have some cookies . . . Oh, you're not fat at all . . . no . . . plump . . . Just leave your umbrella there.

VOICE OF OLD MAN: Follow me, please.

OLD MAN [*back view*]: I have only a modest position . . .

[*The Old Man and Old Woman re-enter together, leaving space between them for their guest. She is invisible. The Old Man and Old Woman advance, downstage, facing the audience and speaking to the invisible Lady, who walks between them.*]

OLD MAN [*to the invisible Lady*]: You've had good weather?

OLD WOMAN [*to the Lady*]: You're not too tired? . . . Yes, a little.

OLD MAN [*to the Lady*]: At the edge of the water . . .

OLD WOMAN [*to the Lady*]: It's kind of you to say so.

OLD MAN [*to the Lady*]: Let me get you a chair.

[*Old Man goes to the left, he exits by door No. 6.*]

OLD WOMAN [*to the Lady*]: Take this one, for the moment,

please. [*She indicates one of the two chairs and seats herself on the other, to the right of the invisible Lady.*] It seems rather warm in here, doesn't it? [*She smiles at the Lady.*] What a charming fan you have! My husband . . . [*The Old Man re-enters through door No. 7, carrying a chair.*] . . . gave me one very like it, that must have been seventy-three years ago . . . and I still have it . . . [*The Old Man places the chair to the left of the invisible Lady.*] . . . it was for my birthday! . . .

[*The Old Man sits on the chair that he has just brought onstage, so that the invisible Lady is between the old couple. The Old Man turns his face towards the Lady, smiles at her, nods his head, softly rubs his hands together, with the air of following what she says. The Old Woman does the same business.*]

OLD MAN: No, madam, life is never cheap.

OLD WOMAN [*to the Lady*]: You are so right . . . [*The Lady speaks.*] As you say, it is about time all that changed . . . [*Changing her tone:*] Perhaps my husband can do something about it . . . he's going to tell you about it.

OLD MAN [*to the Old Woman*]: Hush, hush, Semiramis, the time hasn't come to talk about that yet. [*To the Lady:*] Excuse me, madam, for having aroused your curiosity. [*The Lady reacts.*] Dear madam, don't insist . . .

[*The Old Man and Old Woman smile. They even laugh. They appear to be very amused by the story the invisible Lady tells them. A pause, a moment of silence in the conversation. Their faces lose all expression.*]

OLD MAN [*to the invisible Lady*]: Yes, you're quite right . . .

OLD WOMAN: Yes, yes, yes . . . Oh! surely not.

OLD MAN: Yes, yes, yes. Not at all.

OLD WOMAN: Yes?

OLD MAN: No!?

OLD WOMAN: It's certainly true.

OLD MAN [*laughing*]: It isn't possible.

OLD WOMAN [*laughing*]: Oh! well. [*To the Old Man:*] she's

charming.

OLD MAN [*to the Old Woman*]: Madam has made a conquest. [*To the invisible Lady*:] my congratulations! . . .

OLD WOMAN [*to the invisible Lady*]: You're not like the young people today . . .

OLD MAN [*bending over painfully in order to recover an invisible object that the invisible Lady has dropped*]: Let me . . . don't disturb yourself . . . I'll get it . . . Oh! you're quicker than I . . . [*He straightens up again.*]

OLD WOMAN [*to the Old Man*]: She's younger than you!

OLD MAN [*to the invisible Lady*]: Old age is a heavy burden. I can only wish you an eternal youth.

OLD WOMAN [*to the invisible Lady*]: He's sincere, he speaks from the heart. [*To the Old Man*:] My darling!

[*Several moments of silence. The Old Man and Old Woman, heads turned in profile, look at the invisible Lady, smiling politely; they then turn their heads towards the audience, then look again at the invisible Lady, answering her smile with their smiles, and her questions with their replies.*]

OLD WOMAN: It's very kind of you to take such an interest in us.

OLD MAN: We live a retired life.

OLD WOMAN: My husband's not really misanthropic, he just loves solitude.

OLD MAN: We have the radio, I get in some fishing, and then there's fairly regular boat service.

OLD WOMAN: On Sundays there are two boats in the morning, one in the evening, not to mention privately chartered trips.

OLD MAN [*to the invisible Lady*]: When the weather's clear, there is a moon.

OLD WOMAN [*to the invisible Lady*]: He's always concerned with his duties as general factotum . . . they keep him busy . . . On the other hand, at his age, he might very well take it easy.

OLD MAN [*to the invisible Lady*]: I'll have plenty of time to take it easy in my grave.

OLD WOMAN [*to the Old Man*]: Don't say that, my little darling . . . [*To the invisible Lady*:] Our family, what's left of it, my husband's friends, still came to see us, from time to time, ten years ago . . .

OLD MAN [*to the invisible Lady*]: In the winter, a good book, beside the radiator, and the memories of a lifetime.

OLD WOMAN [*to the invisible Lady*]: A modest life but a full one . . . he devotes two hours every day to work on his message.

[*The doorbell rings. After a short pause, we hear the noise of a boat leaving.*]

OLD WOMAN [*to the Old Man*]: Someone has come. Go quickly.

OLD MAN [*to the invisible Lady*]: Please excuse me, madam. Just a moment! [*To the Old Woman*:] Hurry and bring some chairs!

[*Loud ringing of the doorbell.*]

OLD MAN [*hastening, all bent over, towards door No. 2 to the right, while the Old Woman goes towards the concealed door on the left, hurrying with difficulty, hobbling along*]: It must be someone important. [*He hurries, opens door No. 2, and the invisible Colonel enters. Perhaps it would be useful for us to hear discreetly several trumpet notes, several phrases, like "Hail the Chief." When he opens the door and sees the invisible Colonel, the Old Man stiffens into a respectful position of attention.*] Ah! . . . Colonel! [*He lifts his hand vaguely towards his forehead, so as to roughly sketch a salute.*] Good evening, my dear Colonel . . . This is a very great honor for me . . . I . . . I . . . I was not expecting it . . . although . . . indeed . . . in short, I am most proud to welcome you, a hero of your eminence, into my humble dwelling . . . [*He presses the invisible hand that the invisible Colonel gives him, bending forward ceremoniously, then straightening up again.*] Without false modesty, nevertheless, I permit myself to confess to you that I do not feel unworthy of the honor of your visit! Proud, yes . . . unworthy, no! . . .

[*The Old Woman appears with a chair, entering from the right.*]

OLD WOMAN: Oh! What a handsome uniform! What beautiful medals! Who is it, my darling?

OLD MAN [*to the Old Woman*]: Can't you see that it's the Colonel?

OLD WOMAN [*to the Old Man*]: Ah!

OLD MAN [*to the Old Woman*]: Count his stripes! [*To the Colonel*:] This is my wife, Semiramis. [*To the Old Woman*:] Come here so that I can introduce you to the Colonel. [*The Old Woman approaches, dragging the chair by one hand, and makes a curtsey, without letting go of the chair. To the Colonel*:] My wife. [*To the Old Woman*:] The Colonel.

OLD WOMAN: How do you do, Colonel. Welcome. You're an old comrade of my husband's, he's a general . . .

OLD MAN [*annoyed*]: factotum, factotum . . .

[*The invisible Colonel kisses the hand of the Old Woman. This is apparent from the gesture she makes as she raises her hand toward his lips. Overcome with emotion, the Old Woman lets go of the chair.*]

OLD WOMAN: Oh! He's most polite . . . you can see that he's really superior, a superior being! . . . [*She takes hold of the chair again. To the Colonel*:] This chair is for you . . .

OLD MAN [*to the invisible Colonel*]: This way, if you please . . . [*They move downstage, the Old Woman dragging the chair. To the Colonel*:] Yes, one guest has come already. We're expecting a great many more people! . . .

[*The Old Woman places the chair to the right.*]

OLD WOMAN [*to the Colonel*]: Sit here, please.

[*The Old Man introduces the two invisible guests to each other.*]

OLD MAN: A young lady we know . . .

OLD WOMAN: A very dear friend . . .

OLD MAN [*same business*]: The Colonel . . . a famous soldier.

OLD WOMAN [*indicating the chair she has just brought in to the Colonel*]: Do take this chair . . .

OLD MAN [*to the Old Woman*]: No, no, can't you see that the Colonel wishes to sit beside the Lady! . . .

[*The Colonel seats himself invisibly on the third chair from the left; the invisible Lady is supposedly sitting on the second chair; seated next to each other they engage in an inaudible conversation; the Old Woman and Old Man continue to stand behind their chairs, on both sides of their invisible guests; the Old Man to the left of the Lady, the Old Woman to the right of the Colonel.*]

OLD WOMAN [*listening to the conversation of the two guests*]: Oh! Oh! That's going too far.

OLD MAN [*same business*]: Perhaps. [*The Old Man and the Old Woman make signs to each other over the heads of their guests, while they follow the inaudible conversation which takes a turn that seems to displease them. Abruptly*:] Yes, Colonel, they are not here yet, but they'll be here. And the Orator will speak in my behalf, he will explain the meaning of my message . . . Take care, Colonel, this Lady's husband may arrive at any moment.

OLD WOMAN [*to the Old Man*]: Who is this gentleman?

OLD MAN [*to the Old Woman*]: I've told you, it's the Colonel.

[*Some embarrassing things take place, invisibly.*]

OLD WOMAN [*to the Old Man*]: I knew it. I knew it.

OLD MAN: Then why are you asking?

OLD WOMAN: For my information. Colonel, no cigarette butts on the floor!

OLD MAN [*to Colonel*]: Colonel, Colonel, it's slipped my mind—in the last war did you win or lose?

OLD WOMAN [*to the invisible Lady*]: But my dear, don't let it happen!

OLD MAN: Look at me, look at me, do I look like a bad soldier? One time, Colonel, under fire . . .

OLD WOMAN: He's going too far! It's embarrassing! [*She*

seizes the invisible sleeve of the Colonel.] Listen to him! My darling, why don't you stop him!

OLD MAN [*continuing quickly*]: And all on my own, I killed 209 of them; we called them that because they jumped so high to escape, however there weren't so many of them as there were flies; of course it is less amusing, Colonel, but thanks to my strength of character, I have . . . Oh! no, I must, please.

OLD WOMAN [*to Colonel*]: My husband never lies; it may be true that we are old, nevertheless we're respectable.

OLD MAN [*violently, to the Colonel*]: A hero must be a gentleman too, if he hopes to be a complete hero!

OLD WOMAN [*to the Colonel*]: I've known you for many years, but I'd never have believed you were capable of this. [*To the Lady, while we hear the sound of boats*:] I'd never have believed him capable of this. We have our dignity, our self-respect.

OLD MAN [*in a quavering voice*]: I'm still capable of bearing arms. [*Doorbell rings.*] Excuse me, I must go to the door. [*He stumbles and knocks over the chair of the invisible Lady.*] Oh! pardon.

OLD WOMAN [*rushing forward*]: You didn't hurt yourself? [*The Old Man and Old Woman help the invisible Lady onto her feet.*] You've got all dirty, there's some dust. [*She helps brush the Lady. The doorbell rings again.*]

OLD MAN: Forgive me, forgive me. [*To the Old Woman*:] Go bring a chair.

OLD WOMAN [*to the two invisible guests*]: Excuse me for a moment.

[*While the Old Man goes to open door No. 3, the Old Woman exits through door No. 5 to look for a chair, and she reenters by door No. 8.*]

OLD MAN [*moving towards the door*]: He was trying to get my goat. I'm almost angry. [*He opens the door.*] Oh! madam, you're here! I can scarcely believe my eyes, and yet, nevertheless . . . I didn't really dare to hope . . . really it's . . . Oh! madam, madam . . . I have thought about you, all my life, all my life, madam, they always called you La Belle . . . it's your husband . . . someone told me, certainly . . . you haven't changed a bit . . .Oh! yes, yes, your nose *has* grown longer, maybe it's a little swollen . . . I didn't notice it when I first saw you, but I see it now . . . a lot longer . . . ah! how unfortunate! You certainly didn't do it on purpose . . . how did it happen? . . . little by little . . . excuse me, sir and dear friend, you'll permit me to call you "dear friend," I knew your wife long before you . . . she was the same, but with a completely different nose . . . I congratulate you, sir, you seem to love each other very much. [*The Old Woman re-enters through door No. 8 with a chair.*] Semiramis, two guests have arrived, we need one more chair . . . [*The Old Woman puts the chair behind the four others, then exits by door No. 8 and re-enters by door No. 5, after a few moments, with another chair that she places beside the one she has just brought in. By this time, the Old Man and the two guests have moved near the Old Woman.*] Come this way, please, more guests have arrived. I'm going to introduce you . . . now then, madam . . . Oh! Belle, Belle, Miss Belle, that's what they used to call you . . . now you're all bent over . . . Oh! sir, she is still Belle to me, even so; under her glasses, she still has pretty eyes; her hair is white, but under the white one can see brown, and blue, I'm sure of that . . . come nearer, nearer . . . what is this, sir, a gift, for my wife? [*To the Old Woman, who has just come on with the chair*:] Semiramis, this is Belle, you know, Belle . . . [*To the Colonel and the invisible Lady*:] This is Miss, pardon, Mrs. Belle, don't smile . . . and her husband . . . [*To the Old Woman*:] A childhood friend, I've often spoken of her to you . . . and her husband. [*Again to the Colonel and to the invisible Lady*:] And her husband . . .

OLD WOMAN [*making a little curtsey*]: He certainly makes good introductions. He has fine manners. Good evening, madam, good evening, sir. [*She indicates the two first guests to the newly arrived couple*:] Our friends, yes . . .

OLD MAN [*to the Old Woman*]: He's brought you a present.

[*The Old Woman takes the present.*]

OLD WOMAN: Is it a flower, sir? or a cradle? a pear tree? or a crow?

OLD MAN [*to the Old Woman*]: No, no, can't you see that it's a painting?

OLD WOMAN: Oh! how pretty! Thank you, sir . . . [*To the invisible Lady*:] Would you like to see it, dear friend?

OLD MAN [*to the invisible Colonel*]: Would you like to see it?

OLD WOMAN [*to Belle's husband*]: Doctor, Doctor, I feel squeamish, I have hot flashes, I feel sick, I've aches and pains, I haven't any feeling in my feet, I've caught cold in my eyes, I've a cold in my fingers, I'm suffering from liver trouble, Doctor, Doctor! . . .

OLD MAN [*to the Old Woman*]: This gentleman is not a doctor, he's a photo-engraver.

OLD WOMAN [*to the first invisible Lady*]: If you've finished looking at it, you might hang it up. [*To the Old Man*:] That doesn't matter, he's charming even so, he's dazzling. [*To the Photo-engraver*:] Without meaning to flatter you . . .

[*The Old Man and the Old Woman now move behind the chairs, close to each other, almost touching, but back to back; they talk: the Old Man to Belle, the Old Woman to the Photo-engraver; from time to time their replies, as shown by the way they turn their heads, are addressed to one or the other of the two first guests.*]

OLD MAN [*to Belle*]: I am very touched . . . You're still the same, in spite of everything . . . I've loved you, a hundred years ago . . . But there's been such a change . . . No, you haven't changed a bit . . . I loved you, I love you . . .

OLD WOMAN [*to the Photo-engraver*]: Oh! Sir, sir, sir . . .

OLD MAN [*to the Colonel*]: I'm in complete agreement with you on that point.

OLD WOMAN [*to the Photo-engraver*]: Oh! certainly, sir, certainly, sir, certainly . . . [*To the first Lady*:] Thanks for hanging it up . . . Forgive me if I've inconvenienced you.

[*The light grows stronger. It should grow stronger and stronger as the invisible guests continue to arrive.*]

OLD MAN [*almost whimpering to Belle*]: Where are the snows of yester year?

OLD WOMAN [*to the Photo-engraver*]: Oh! Sir, sir, sir . . . Oh! sir . . .

OLD MAN [*pointing out the first lady to Belle*]: She's a young friend . . . she's very sweet . . .

OLD WOMAN [*pointing the Colonel out to the Photo-engraver*]: Yes, he's a mounted staff colonel . . . a comrade of my husband . . . a subaltern, my husband's a general . . .

OLD MAN [*to Belle*]: Your ears were not always so pointed! . . . My Belle, do you remember?

OLD WOMAN [*to the Photo-engraver, simpering grotesquely; she develops this manner more and more in this scene; she shows her thick red stockings, raises her many petticoats, shows an underskirt full of holes, exposes her old breast; then, her hands on her hips, throws her head back, makes little erotic cries, projects her pelvis, her legs spread apart; she laughs like an old prostitute; this business, entirely different from her manner heretofore as well as from that she will have subsequently, and which must reveal the hidden personality of the Old Woman, ceases abruptly*]: So you think I'm too old for that, do you?

OLD MAN [*to Belle, very romantically*]: When we were young, the moon was a living star, Ah! yes, yes, if only we had dared, but we were only children. Wouldn't you like to recapture those bygone days . . . is it still possible? Is it still possible? Ah! no, no, it is no longer possible. Those days have flown away as fast as a train. Time has left the marks of his wheels on our skin. Do you believe surgeons can perform miracles? [*To the Colonel*:] I am a soldier, and you too, we soldiers are always young, the generals are like gods . . . [*To Belle*:] It ought to be that way . . . Alas! Alas! We have lost everything. We could have been so happy, I'm sure of it, we could have been, we could have been; perhaps the flowers are budding again beneath the snow! . . .

OLD WOMAN [*to Photo-engraver*]: Flatterer! Rascal! Ah! Ah! I look younger than my years? You're a little savage! You're exciting.

OLD MAN [*to Belle*]: Will you be my Isolde and let me be your Tristan? Beauty is more than skin deep, it's in the heart . . . Do you understand? We could have had the pleasure of sharing, joy, beauty, eternity . . . an eternity . . . Why didn't we dare? We weren't brave enough . . . Everything is lost, lost, lost.

OLD WOMAN [*to Photo-engraver*]: Oh no, Oh! no, Oh! la la, you give me the shivers. You too, are you ticklish? To tickle or be tickled? I'm a little embarrassed . . . [*She laughs.*] Do you like my petticoat? Or do you like this skirt better?

OLD MAN [*to Belle*]: A general factotum has a poor life!

OLD WOMAN [*turning her head towards the first invisible Lady*]: In order to make crepes de Chine? A leaf of beef, an hour of flour, a little gastric sugar. [*To the Photo-engraver*:] You've got clever fingers, ah . . . all the sa-a-a-me! . . . Oh-oh-oh-oh.

OLD MAN [*to Belle*]: My worthy helpmeet, Semiramis, has taken the place of my mother. [*He turns towards the Colonel*:] Colonel, as I've often observed to you, one must take the truth as one finds it. [*He turns back towards Belle.*]

OLD WOMAN [*to Photo-engraver*]: Do you really really believe that one could have children at any age? Any age children?

OLD MAN [*to Belle*]: It's this alone that has saved me: the inner life, peace of mind, austerity, my scientific investigations, philosophy, my message . . .

OLD WOMAN [*to Photo-engraver*]: I've never yet betrayed my

husband, the general . . . not so hard, you're going to make me fall . . . I'm only his poor mamma! [*She sobs.*] A great, great [*She pushes him back.*], great . . . mamma. My conscience causes these tears to flow. For me the branch of the apple tree is broken. Try to find somebody else. I no longer want to gather rosebuds . . .

OLD MAN [*to Belle*]: . . . All the preoccupations of a superior order . . .

[*The Old Man and Old Woman lead Belle and the Photo-engraver up alongside the two other invisible guests, and seat them.*]

OLD MAN AND OLD WOMAN [*to the Photo-engraver and Belle*]: Sit down, please sit down.

[*The Old Man and Old Woman sit down too, he to the left, she to the right, with the four empty chairs between them. A long mute scene, punctuated at intervals with "no," "yes," "yes." The Old Man and Old Woman listen to the conversation of the invisible guests.*]

OLD WOMAN [*to the Photo-engraver*]: We had one son . . . of course, he's still alive . . . he's gone away . . . it's a common story . . . or, rather, unusual . . . he abandoned his parents . . . he had a heart of gold . . . that was a long time ago . . . We loved him so much . . . he slammed the door . . . My husband and I tried to hold him back with all our might . . . he was seven years old, the age of reason, I called after him: "My son, my child, my son, my child." . . . He didn't even look back . . .

OLD MAN: Alas, no . . . no, we've never had a child . . .I'd hoped for a son . . . Semiramis, too . . . we did everything . . . and my poor Semiramis is so maternal, too. Perhaps it was better that way . . . As for me I was an ungrateful son myself . . . Ah! . . . grief, regret, remorse, that's all we have . . . that's all we have left . . .

OLD WOMAN: He said to me: "You kill birds! Why do you kill birds?" . . . But we don't kill birds . . . we've never harmed so much as a fly . . . His eyes were full of big tears.

He wouldn't let us dry them. He wouldn't let me come near him. He said: "Yes, you kill all the birds, all the birds." . . . He showed us his little fists . . . "You're lying, you've betrayed me! The streets are full of dead birds, of dying baby birds." It's the song of the birds! . . . "No, it's their death rattle. The sky is red with blood." . . . No, my child, it's blue. He cried again: "You've betrayed me, I adored you, I believed you to be good . . . the streets are full of dead birds, you've torn out their eyes . . . Papa, mamma, you're wicked! . . . I refuse to stay with you." . . . I threw myself at his feet . . . His father was weeping. We couldn't hold him back. As he went we could still hear him calling: "It's you who are responsible" . . . What does that mean, "responsible"?

OLD MAN: I let my mother die all alone in a ditch. She called after me, moaning feebly: "My little child, my beloved son, don't leave me to die all alone . . . Stay with me. I don't have much time left." Don't worry, Mamma, I told her, I'll be back in a moment . . . I was in a hurry . . . I was going to the ball, to dance. I will be back in a minute. But when I returned, she was already dead, and they had buried her deep . . . I broke open the grave, I searched for her . . . I couldn't find her . . . I know, I know, sons, always, abandon their mothers, and they more or less kill their fathers . . . Life is like that . . . but I, I suffer from it . . . and the others, they don't . . .

OLD WOMAN: He cried: "Papa, Mamma, I'll never set eyes on you again."

OLD MAN: I suffer from it, yes, the others don't . . .

OLD WOMAN: Don't speak of him to my husband. He loved his parents so much. He never left them for a single moment. He cared for them, coddled them . . . And they died in his arms, saying to him: "You have been a perfect son. God will be good to you."

OLD MAN: I can still see her stretched out in the ditch, she was holding lily of the valley in her hand, she cried: "Don't forget me, don't forget me" . . . her eyes were full of big tears, and she called me by my baby name: "Little Chick," she said, "Little Chick, don't leave me here all alone."

OLD WOMAN [*to the Photo-engraver*]: He has never written to us. From time to time, a friend tells us that he's been seen here or there, that he is well, that he is a good husband . . .

OLD MAN [*to Belle*]: When I got back, she had been buried a long time. [*To the first invisible Lady*:] Oh, yes. Oh! yes, madam, we have a movie theatre in the house, a restaurant, bathrooms . . .

OLD WOMAN [*to the Colonel*]: Yes, Colonel, it is because he . . .

OLD MAN: Basically that's it.

[*Desultory conversation, getting bogged down.*]

OLD WOMAN: If only!

OLD MAN: Thus, I've not . . . I, it . . . certainly . . .

OLD WOMAN [*dislocated dialogue, exhaustion*]: All in all.

OLD MAN: To ours and to theirs.

OLD WOMAN: So that.

OLD MAN: From me to him.

OLD WOMAN: Him, or her?

OLD MAN: Them.

OLD WOMAN: Curl-papers . . . After all.

OLD MAN: It's not that.

OLD WOMAN: Why?

OLD MAN: Yes.

OLD WOMAN: I.

OLD MAN: All in all.

OLD WOMAN: All in all.

OLD MAN [*to the first invisible Lady*]: What was that, madam?

[*A long silence, the Old Man and Old Woman remain rigid on their chairs. Then the doorbell rings.*]

OLD MAN [*with increasing nervousness*]: Someone has come. People. Still more people.

OLD WOMAN: I thought I heard some boats.

OLD MAN: I'll go to the door. Go bring some chairs. Excuse me, gentlemen, ladies. [*He goes towards door No. 7.*]

OLD WOMAN [*to the invisible guests who have already arrived*]: Get up for a moment, please. The Orator will be here soon. We must ready the room for the meeting. [*The Old Woman arranges the chairs, turning their backs towards the audience.*] Lend me a hand, please. Thanks.

OLD MAN [*opening door No. 7*]: Good evening, ladies, good evening, gentlemen. Please come in.

[*The three or four invisible persons who have arrived are very tall, and the Old Man has to stand on his toes in order to shake hands with them. The Old Woman, after placing the chairs as indicated above, goes over to the Old Man.*]

OLD MAN [*making introductions*]: My wife . . . Mr. . . . Mrs. . . . my wife . . . Mr. . . . Mrs. . . . my wife . . .

OLD WOMAN: Who are all these people, my darling?

OLD MAN [*to Old Woman*]: Go find some chairs, dear.

OLD WOMAN: I can't do everything! . . .

[*She exits, grumbling, by door No. 6 and re-enters by door No. 7, while the Old Man, with the newly arrived guests, moves downstage.*]

OLD MAN: Don't drop your movie camera. [*More introductions.*] The Colonel . . . the Lady . . . Mrs. Belle . . . the Photo-engraver . . . These are the newspaper men, they have come to hear the Orator too, who should be here any minute now . . . Don't be impatient . . . You'll not be bored . . . all together now . . . [*The Old Woman re-enters through door No. 7 with two chairs.*] Come along, bring the chairs more quickly . . . we're still short one.

[*The Old Woman goes to find another chair, still grumbling, exiting by door No. 3, and re-entering by door No. 8.*]

OLD WOMAN: All right, and so . . . I'm doing as well as I can . . . I'm not a machine, you know . . . Who are all these people? [*She exits.*]

OLD MAN: Sit down, sit down, the ladies with the ladies, and the gentlemen with the gentlemen, or vice versa, if you prefer . . . We don't have any more nice chairs . . . we have to make do with what we have . . . I'm sorry . . . take the one in the middle . . . does anyone need a fountain pen? Telephone Maillot, you'll get Monique . . . Claude is an angel. I don't have a radio . . . I take all the newspapers . . . that depends on a number of things; I manage these buildings, but I have no help . . . we have to economize . . . no interviews, please, for the moment . . . later, we'll see . . . you'll soon have a place to sit . . . what can she be doing? [*The Old Woman enters by door No. 8 with a chair.*] Faster, Semiramis . . .

OLD WOMAN: I'm doing my best . . . Who are all these people?

OLD MAN: I'll explain it all to you later.

OLD WOMAN: And that woman? That woman, my darling?

OLD MAN: Don't get upset . . . [*To the Colonel:*] Colonel, journalism is a profession too, like a fighting man's . . . [*To the Old Woman:*] Take care of the ladies, my dear . . . [*The doorbell rings. The Old Man hurries towards door No. 8.*] Wait a moment . . . [*To the Old Woman:*] Bring chairs!

OLD WOMAN: Gentlemen, ladies, excuse me . . .

[*She exits by door No. 3, re-entering by door No. 2; the Old Man goes to open concealed door No. 9, and disappears at the moment the Old Woman re-enters by door No. 2.*]

OLD MAN [*out of sight*]: Come in . . . come in . . . come in . . . come in . . . [*He reappears, leading in a number of invisible people, including one very small child he holds by the hand.*] One doesn't bring little children to a scientific lecture . . . the poor little thing is going to be bored . . . if he begins to cry or to peepee on the ladies' dresses, that'll be a fine state of affairs! [*He conducts them to stage center; the Old Woman comes on with two chairs.*] I wish to introduce you to my wife, Semiramis; and these are their children.

OLD WOMAN: Ladies, gentlemen . . . Oh! aren't they sweet!

OLD MAN: That one is the smallest.

OLD WOMAN: Oh, he's so cute . . . so cute . . . so cute!

OLD MAN: Not enough chairs.

OLD WOMAN: Oh! dear, oh dear, oh dear . . .

[*She exits, looking for another chair, using now door No. 2 as exit and door No. 3 on the right to re-enter.*]

OLD MAN: Hold the little boy on your lap . . . The twins can sit together in the same chair. Be careful, they're not very strong . . . they go with the house, they belong to the landlord. Yes, my children, he'd make trouble for us, he's a bad man . . . he wants us to buy them from him, these worthless chairs. [*The Old Woman returns as quickly as she can with a chair.*] You don't all know each other . . . you're seeing each other for the first time . . . you knew each other by name . . . [*To the Old Woman:*] Semiramis, help me make the introductions . . .

OLD WOMAN: Who are all these people? . . . May I introduce you, excuse me . . . May I introduce you . . . but who are they?

OLD MAN: May I introduce you . . . Allow me to introduce you . . . permit me to introduce you . . . Mr., Mrs., Miss . . . Mr. . . . Mrs. . . . Mrs. . . . Mr.

OLD WOMAN [*to Old Man*]: Did you put on your sweater? [*To the invisible guests:*] Mr., Mrs., Mr. . . .

[*Doorbell rings again.*]

OLD MAN: More people!

[*Another ring of doorbell.*]

OLD WOMAN: More people!

[*The doorbell rings again, then several more times, and more times again; the Old Man is beside himself; the chairs, turned towards the dais, with their backs to the audience, form regular rows, each one longer as in a theatre; the Old Man is winded, he mops his brow, goes from one door to another, seats invisible people, while the Old Woman, hob-*

bling along, unable to move any faster, goes as rapidly as she can, from one door to another, hunting for chairs and carrying them in. There are now many invisible people on stage; both the Old Man and Old Woman take care not to bump into people and to thread their way between the rows of chairs. The movement could go like this: the Old Man goes to door No. 4, the Old Woman exits by door No. 3, returns by door No. 2; the Old Man goes to open door No. 7, the Old Woman exits by door No. 8, re-enters by door No. 6 with chairs, etc., in this manner making their way around the stage, using all the doors.]

OLD WOMAN: Beg pardon . . . excuse me . . . what . . . oh, yes . . . beg pardon . . . excuse me . . .

OLD MAN: Gentlemen . . . come in . . . ladies . . . enter . . . it is Mrs. . . . let me . . . yes . . .

OLD WOMAN [*with more chairs*]: Oh dear . . . Oh dear . . . there are too many . . . There really are too, too . . . too many, oh dear, oh dear, oh dear . . .

[*We hear from outside, louder and louder and approaching nearer and nearer, the sounds of boats moving through the water; all the noises come directly from the wings. The Old Woman and the Old Man continue the business outlined above; they open the doors, they carry in chairs. The doorbell continues to ring.*]

OLD MAN: This table is in our way. [*He moves a table, or he sketches the business of moving it, without slowing down his rhythm, aided by the Old Woman.*] There's scarcely a place left here, excuse us . . .

OLD WOMAN [*making a gesture of clearing the table, to the Old Man*]: Are you wearing your sweater?

[*Doorbell rings.*]

OLD MAN: More people! More chairs! More people! More chairs! Come in, come in, ladies and gentlemen . . . Semiramis, faster . . . We'll give you a hand soon . . .

OLD WOMAN: Beg pardon . . . beg pardon . . . good evening, Mrs. . . . Mrs. . . . Mr. . . . Mr. . . . yes, yes, the chairs . . .

[*The doorbell rings louder and louder and we hear the noises of boats striking the quay very close by, and more and more frequently. The Old Man flounders among the chairs; he has scarcely enough time to go from one door to another, so rapidly do the ringings of the doorbell succeed each other.*]

OLD MAN: Yes, right away . . . are you wearing your sweater? Yes, yes . . . immediately, patience, yes, yes . . . patience . . .

OLD WOMAN: Your sweater? My sweater? . . . Beg pardon, beg pardon.

OLD MAN: This way, ladies and gentlemen, I request you . . . I re you . . . pardon . . . quest . . . enter, enter . . . going to show . . . there, the seats . . . dear friend . . . not there . . . take care . . . you, my friend?

[*Then a long moment without words. We hear waves, boats, the continuous ringing of the doorbell. The movement culminates in intensity at this point. The doors are now opening and shutting all together ceaselessly. Only the main door in the center of the recess remains closed. The Old Man and Old Woman come and go, without saying a word, from one door to another; they appear to be gliding on roller skates. The Old Man receives the people, accompanies them, but doesn't take them very far, he only indicates seats to them after having taken one or two steps with them; he hasn't enough time. The Old Woman carries in chairs. The Old Man and the Old Woman meet each other and bump into each other, once or twice, without interrupting their rhythm. Then, the Old Man takes a position upstage center, and turns from left to right, from right to left, etc., towards all the doors and indicates the seats with his arms. His arms move very rapidly. Then, finally the Old Woman stops, with a chair in one hand, which she places, takes up again, replaces, looks as though she, too, wants to go from one door to another, from right to left, from left to right, moving her head and neck very rapidly. This must not interrupt the rhythm; the Old Man and Old Woman must still give the impression of not stopping, even while remaining almost in one place; their hands, their chests, their heads, their eyes are agitated, perhaps moving in little circles. Finally, there is a progressive slowing down of movement, at first slight: the ringings of the doorbell are less loud, less frequent; the doors open less and less rapidly; the gestures of the Old Man and Old Woman slacken continuously. At the moment when the doors stop opening and closing altogether, and the ringings cease to be heard, we have the impression that the stage is packed with people.*]

OLD MAN: I'm going to find a place for you . . . patience . . . Semiramis, for the love of . . .

OLD WOMAN [*with a large gesture, her hands empty*]: There are no more chairs, my darling. [*Then, abruptly, she begins to sell invisible programs in a full hall, with the doors closed.*] Programs, get your programs here, the program of the evening, buy your program!

OLD MAN: Relax, ladies and gentlemen, we'll take care of you . . . Each in his turn, in the order of your arrival . . . You'll have a seat. I'll take care of you.

OLD WOMAN: Buy your programs! Wait a moment, madam, I cannot take care of everyone at the same time, I haven't got thirty-three hands, you know, I'm not a cow . . . Mister, please be kind enough to pass the program to the lady next to you, thank you . . . my change, my change . . .

OLD MAN: I've told you that I'd find a place for you! Don't get excited! Over here, it's over here, there, take care . . . oh, dear friend . . . dear friends . . .

OLD WOMAN: . . . Programs . . . get your grams . . . grams . . .

OLD MAN: Yes, my dear, she's over there, further down, she's selling programs . . . no trade is unworthy . . . that's her . . . do you see her? . . . you have a seat in the second row . . . to the right . . . no, to the left . . . that's it! . . .

OLD WOMAN: . . . gram . . . gram . . . program . . . get your program . . .

OLD MAN: What do you expect me to do? I'm doing my best! [*To invisible seated people*:] Push over a little, if you will please . . . there's still a little room, that will do for you, won't it, Mrs. . . . come here. [*He mounts the dais, forced by the pushing of the crowd.*] Ladies, gentlemen, please excuse us, there are no more seats available . . .

OLD WOMAN [*who is now on the opposite side of the stage, across from the Old Man, between door No. 3 and the window*]: Get your programs . . . who wants a program? Eskimo pies, caramels . . . fruit drops . . . [*Unable to move, the Old Woman, hemmed in by the crowd, scatters her programs and candies anywhere, above the invisible heads.*] Here are some! There they are!

OLD MAN [*standing on the dais, very animated; he is jostled as he descends from the dais, remounts it, steps down again, hits someone in the face, is struck by an elbow, says*]: Pardon . . . please excuse us . . . take care . . . [*Pushed, he staggers, has trouble regaining his equilibrium, clutches at shoulders.*]

OLD WOMAN: Why are there so many people? Programs, get your program here, Eskimo pies.

OLD MAN: Ladies, young ladies, gentlemen, a moment of silence, I beg you . . . silence . . . it's very important . . . those people who've no seats are asked to clear the aisles . . . that's it . . . don't stand between the chairs.

OLD WOMAN [*to the Old Man, almost screaming*]: Who are all these people, my darling? What are they doing here?

OLD MAN: Clear the aisles, ladies and gentlemen. Those who do not have seats must, for the convenience of all, stand against the wall, there, along the right or the left . . . you'll be able to hear everything, you'll see everything, don't worry, you won't miss a thing, all seats are equally good!

[*There is a great hullabaloo. Pushed by the crowd, the Old Man makes almost a complete turn around the stage and ends up at the window on the right, near to the stool. The Old Woman makes the same movement in reverse, and ends up at the window on the left, near the stool there.*]

OLD MAN [*making this movement*]: Don't push, don't push.

OLD WOMAN [*same business*]: Don't push, don't push.

OLD MAN [*same business*]: Don't push, don't push.

OLD WOMAN [*same business*]: Don't push, ladies and gentlemen, don't push.

OLD MAN [*same business*]: Relax . . . take it easy . . . be quiet . . . what's going on here?

OLD WOMAN [*same business*]: There's no need to act like savages, in any case.

[*At last they reach their final positions. Each is near a window. The Old Man to the left, by the window which is beside the dais. The Old Woman on the right. They don't move from these positions until the end.*]

OLD WOMAN [*calling to the Old Man*]: My darling . . . I can't see you, anymore . . . where are you? Who are they? What do all these people want? Who is that man over there?

OLD MAN: Where are you? Where are you, Semiramis?

OLD WOMAN: My darling, where are you?

OLD MAN: Here, beside the window . . . Can you hear me?

OLD WOMAN: Yes, I hear your voice! . . . there are so many . . . but I can make out yours . . .

OLD MAN: And you, where are you?

OLD WOMAN: I'm beside the window too! . . . My dear, I'm frightened, there are too many people . . . we are very far from each other . . . at our age we have to be careful . . . we might get lost . . . We must stay close together, one never knows, my darling, my darling . . .

OLD MAN: Ah! . . . I just caught sight of you . . . Oh! . . . We'll find each other, never fear . . . I'm with friends. [*To the friends*:] I'm happy to shake your hands . . . But of course, I believe in progress, uninterrupted progress, with some jolts, nevertheless . . .

OLD WOMAN: That's fine, thanks . . . What foul weather! Yes, it's been nice! [*Aside*:] I'm afraid, even so . . . What am I doing here? . . . [*She screams*:] My darling, My darling!

[*The Old Man and Old Woman individually speak to guests near them.*]

OLD MAN: In order to prevent the exploitation of man by man, we need money, money, and still more money!

OLD WOMAN: My darling! [*Then, hemmed in by friends*:] Yes, my husband is here, he's organizing everything . . . over there . . . Oh! you'll never get there . . . you'd have to go across, he's with friends . . .

OLD MAN: Certainly not . . . as I've always said . . . pure logic does not exist . . . all we've got is an imitation.

OLD WOMAN: But you know, there are people who are happy. In the morning they eat breakfast on the plane, at noon they lunch in the pullman, and in the evening they dine aboard the liner. At night they sleep in the trucks that roll, roll, roll . . .

OLD MAN: Talk about the dignity of man! At least let's try to save face. Dignity is only skin deep.

OLD WOMAN: Don't slink away into the shadows . . . [*She bursts out laughing in conversation.*]

OLD MAN: Your compatriots ask of me.

OLD WOMAN: Certainly . . . tell me everything.

OLD MAN: I've invited you . . . in order to explain to you . . . that the individual and the person are one and the same.

OLD WOMAN: He has a borrowed look about him. He owes us a lot of money.

OLD MAN: I am not myself. I am another. I am the one in the other.

OLD WOMAN: My children, take care not to trust one another.

OLD MAN: Sometimes I awaken in the midst of absolute silence. It's a perfect circle. There's nothing lacking. But one must be careful, all the same. Its shape might disappear. There are holes through which it can escape.

OLD WOMAN: Ghosts, you know, phantoms, mere nothings . . . The duties my husband fulfills are very important, sublime.

OLD MAN: Excuse me . . . that's not at all my opinion! At the proper time, I'll communicate my views on this subject to you . . . I have nothing to say for the present! . . . We're waiting for the Orator, he'll tell you, he'll speak in my behalf, and explain everything that we hold most dear . . . he'll explain everything to you . . . when? . . . when the moment has come . . . the moment will come soon . . .

OLD WOMAN [*on her side to her friends*]: The sooner, the better . . . That's understood . . . [*Aside*:] They're never going to leave us alone. Let them go, why don't they go? . . . My poor darling, where is he? I can't see him any more . . .

OLD MAN [*same business*]: Don't be so impatient. You'll hear my message. In just a moment.

OLD WOMAN [*aside*]: Ah! . . . I hear his voice! . . . [*To her friends*:] Do you know, my husband has never been understood. But at last his hour has come.

OLD MAN: Listen to me, I've had a rich experience of life. In all walks of life, at every level of thought . . . I'm not an egotist: humanity must profit by what I've learned.

OLD WOMAN: Ow! You stepped on my foot . . . I've got chilblains!

OLD MAN: I've perfected a real system. [*Aside*:] The Orator ought to be here. [*Aloud*:] I've suffered enormously.

OLD WOMAN: We have suffered so much. [*Aside*:] The Orator ought to be here. It's certainly time.

OLD MAN: Suffered much, learned much.

OLD WOMAN [*like an echo*]: Suffered much, learned much.

OLD MAN: You'll see for yourselves, my system is perfect.

OLD WOMAN [*like an echo*]: You'll see for yourselves, his system is perfect.

OLD MAN: If only my instructions are carried out.

OLD WOMAN [*echo*]: If only his instructions are carried out.

OLD MAN: We'll save the world! . . .

OLD WOMAN [*echo*]: Saving his own soul by saving the world! . . .

OLD MAN: One truth for all!

OLD WOMAN [*echo*]: One truth for all!

OLD MAN: Follow me! . . .

OLD WOMAN [*echo*]: Follow him! . . .

OLD MAN: For I have absolute certainty! . . .

OLD WOMAN [*echo*]: He has absolute certainty!

OLD MAN: Never . . .

OLD WOMAN [*echo*]: Ever and ever . . .

[*Suddenly we hear noises in the wings, fanfares.*]

OLD WOMAN: What's going on?

[*The noises increase, then the main door opens wide, with a great crash; through the open door we see nothing but a very powerful light which floods onto the stage through the main door and the windows, which at the entrance of the emperor are brightly lighted.*]

OLD MAN: I don't know . . . I can scarcely believe . . . is it possible . . . but yes . . . but yes . . . incredible . . . and still it's true . . . yes . . . if . . . yes . . . it is the Emperor! His Majesty the Emperor!

[*The light reaches its maximum intensity, through the open door and through the windows; but the light is cold, empty; more noises which cease abruptly.*]

OLD MAN: Stand up! . . . It's His Majesty the Emperor! The Emperor in my house, in our house . . . Semiramis . . . do you realize what this means?

OLD WOMAN [*not understanding*]: The Emperor . . . the Emperor? My darling! [*Then suddenly she understands.*] Ah, yes, the Emperor! Your Majesty! Your Majesty! [*She wildly makes countless grotesque curtsies.*] In our house! In our house!

OLD MAN [*weeping with emotion*]: Your Majesty! . . . Oh! Your Majesty! . . . Your little, Your great Majesty! . . . Oh! what a sublime honor . . . it's all a marvelous dream.

OLD WOMAN [*like an echo*]: A marvelous dream . . . arvelous . . .

OLD MAN [*to the invisible crowd*]: Ladies, gentlemen, stand up, our beloved sovereign, the Emperor, is among us! Hurrah! Hurrah!

[*He stands up on the stool; he stands on his toes in order to see the Emperor; the Old Woman does the same on her side.*]

OLD WOMAN: Hurrah! Hurrah!

[*Stamping of feet.*]

OLD MAN: Your Majesty! . . . I'm over here! . . . Your Majesty! Can you hear me? Can you see me? Please tell his Majesty that I'm here! Your Majesty! Your Majesty!!! I'm here, your most faithful servant! . . .

OLD WOMAN [*still echoing*]: Your most faithful servant, Your Majesty!

OLD MAN: Your servant, your slave, your dog, arf, arf, your dog, Your Majesty! . . .

OLD WOMAN [*barking loudly like a dog*]: Arf . . . arf . . . arf . . .

OLD MAN [*wringing his hands*]: Can you see me? . . . Answer, Sire! . . . Ah, I can see you, I've just caught sight of Your Majesty's august face . . . your divine forehead . . . I've seen you, yes, in spite of the screen of courtiers . . .

OLD WOMAN: In spite of the courtiers . . . we're here, Your Majesty!

OLD MAN: Your Majesty! Your Majesty! Ladies, gentlemen, don't keep him—His Majesty standing . . . you see, Your Majesty, I'm truly the only one who cares for you, for your health, I'm the most faithful of all your subjects . . .

OLD WOMAN [*echoing*]: Your Majesty's most faithful subjects!

OLD MAN: Let me through, now, ladies and gentlemen . . . how can I make my way through such a crowd? . . . I must go to present my most humble respects to His Majesty, the Emperor . . . let me pass . . .

OLD WOMAN [*echo*]: Let him pass . . . let him pass . . . pass . . . ass . . .

OLD MAN: Let me pass, please, let me pass. [*Desperate*:] Ah! Will I ever be able to reach him?

OLD WOMAN [*echo*]: Reach him . . . reach him . . .

OLD MAN: Nevertheless, my heart and my whole being are at his feet, the crowd of courtiers surrounds him, ah! ah! they want to prevent me from approaching him . . . They know very well that . . . oh! I understand, I understand . . . Court intrigues, I know all about it . . . They hope to separate me from Your Majesty!

OLD WOMAN: Calm yourself, my darling . . . His Majesty sees you, he's looking at you . . . His Majesty has given me a wink . . . His Majesty is on our side! . . .

OLD MAN: They must give the Emperor the best seat . . . near the dais . . . so that he can hear everything the Orator is going to say.

OLD WOMAN [*hoisting herself up on the stool, on her toes, lifting her chin as high as she can, in order to see better*]: At last they're taking care of the Emperor.

OLD MAN: Thank heaven for that! [*To the Emperor*:] Sire . . . Your Majesty may rely on him. It's my friend, it's my representative who is at Your Majesty's side. [*On his toes, standing on the stool*:] Gentlemen, ladies, young ladies, little children, I implore you.

OLD WOMAN [*echoing*]: Plore . . . plore . . .

OLD MAN: . . . I want to see . . . move aside . . . I want . . . the celestial gaze, the noble face, the crown, the radiance of His Majesty . . . Sire, deign to turn your illustrious face in my direction, toward your humble servant . . . so humble . . . Oh! I caught sight of him clearly that time . . . I caught sight . . .

OLD WOMAN [*echo*]: He caught sight that time . . . he caught sight . . . caught . . . sight . . .

OLD MAN: I'm at the height of joy . . . I've no more words to express my boundless gratitude . . . in my humble dwelling, Oh! Majesty! Oh! radiance! . . . here . . . here . . . in the dwelling where I am, true enough, a general . . . but within the hierarchy of your army, I'm only a simple general factotum . . .

OLD WOMAN [*echo*]: General factotum . . .

OLD MAN: I'm proud of it . . . proud and humble, at the same time . . . as I should be . . . alas! certainly, I am a general, I might have been at the imperial court, I have only a little court here to take care of . . . Your Majesty . . . I . . . Your Majesty, I have difficulty expressing myself . . . I might have had . . . many things, not a few possessions if I'd known, if I'd wanted, if I . . . if we . . . Your Majesty, forgive my emotion . . .

OLD WOMAN: Speak in the third person!

OLD MAN [*sniveling*]: May Your Majesty deign to forgive me! You are here at last . . . We had given up hope . . . you might not even have come . . . Oh! Savior, in my life, I have been humiliated . . .

OLD WOMAN [*echo, sobbing*]: . . . miliated . . . miliated . . .

OLD MAN: I've suffered much in my life . . . I might have been something, if I could have been sure of the support of Your Majesty . . . I have no other support . . . if you hadn't come, everything would have been too late . . . you are, Sire, my last recourse . . .

OLD WOMAN [*echo*]: Last recourse . . . Sire . . . ast recourse . . . ire . . . recourse . . .

OLD MAN: I've brought bad luck to my friends, to all those who have helped me . . . Lightning struck the hand which was held out toward me . . .

OLD WOMAN [*echo*]: . . . hand that was held out . . . held out . . . out . . .

OLD MAN: They've always had good reasons for hating me, bad reasons for loving me . . .

OLD WOMAN: That's not true, my darling, not true. *I* love you, I'm your little mother . . .

OLD MAN: All my enemies have been rewarded and my friends have betrayed me . . .

OLD WOMAN [*echo*]: Friends . . . betrayed . . . betrayed . . .

OLD MAN: They've treated me badly. They've persecuted me. If I complained, it was always they who were in the right . . . Sometimes I've tried to revenge myself . . . I was never able to, never able to revenge myself . . . I have too much pity . . . I refused to strike the enemy to the ground, I have always been too good.

OLD WOMAN [*echo*]: He was too good, good, good, good, good . . .

OLD MAN: It is my pity that has defeated me.

OLD WOMAN [*echo*]: My pity . . . pity . . . pity . . .

OLD MAN: But they never pitied me. I gave them a pin prick, and they repaid me with club blows, with knife blows, with cannon blows, they've crushed my bones . . .

OLD WOMAN [*echo*]: . . . My bones . . . my bones . . . my bones . . .

OLD MAN: They've supplanted me, they've robbed me, they've assassinated me . . . I've been the collector of injustices, the lightning rod of catastrophes . . .

OLD WOMAN [*echo*]: Lightning rod . . . catastrophe . . . lightning rod . . .

OLD MAN: In order to forget, Your Majesty, I wanted to go in for sports . . . for mountain climbing . . . they pulled my feet and made me slip . . . I wanted to climb stairways, they rotted the steps . . . I fell down . . . I wanted to travel, they refused me a passport . . . I wanted to cross the river, they burnt my bridges . . .

OLD WOMAN [*echo*]: Burnt my bridges.

OLD MAN: I wanted to cross the Pyrenees, and there were no more Pyrenees.

OLD WOMAN [*echo*]: No more Pyrenees . . . He could have been, he too, Your Majesty, like so many others, a head editor, a head actor, a head doctor, Your Majesty, a head king . . .

OLD MAN: Furthermore, no one has ever shown me due consideration . . . no one has ever sent me invitations . . . However, I, hear me, I say this to you, I alone could have saved humanity, who is so sick. Your Majesty realizes this as do I . . . or, at the least, I could have spared it the evils from which it has suffered so much this last quarter of a century, had I had the opportunity to communicate my message; I do not despair of saving it, there is still time, I have a plan . . . alas, I express myself with difficulty . . .

OLD WOMAN [*above the invisible heads*]: The Orator will be here, he'll speak for you. His Majesty is here, thus you'll be heard, you've no reason to despair, you hold all the trumps, everything has changed, everything has changed . . .

OLD MAN: I hope Your Majesty will excuse me . . . I know you have many other worries . . . I've been humiliated . . . Ladies and gentlemen, move aside just a little bit, don't hide His Majesty's nose from me altogether, I want to see the diamonds of the imperial crown glittering . . . But if Your Majesty has deigned to come to our miserable home, it is because you have condescended to take into consideration my wretched self. What an extraordinary reward. Your Majesty, if corporeally I raise myself on my toes, this is not through pride, this is only in order to gaze upon you! . . . morally, I throw myself at your knees.

OLD WOMAN [*sobbing*]: At your knees, Sire, we throw ourselves at your knees, at your feet, at your toes . . .

OLD MAN: I've had scabies. My employer fired me because I did not bow to his baby, to his horse. I've been kicked in the ass, but all this, Sire, no longer has any importance . . . since . . . since . . . Sir . . . Your Majesty . . . look . . . I am here . . . here . . .

OLD WOMAN [*echo*]: Here . . . here . . . here . . . here . . . here . . . here . . .

OLD MAN: Since Your Majesty is here . . . since Your Majesty will take my message into consideration . . . But the Orator should be here . . . he's making His Majesty wait . . .

OLD WOMAN: If Your Majesty will forgive him. He's surely coming. He will be here in a moment. They've telephoned us.

OLD MAN: His Majesty is so kind. His Majesty wouldn't depart just like that, without having listened to everything, heard everything.

OLD WOMAN [*echo*]: Heard everything . . . heard . . . listened to everything . . .

OLD MAN: It is he who will speak in my name . . . I, I cannot . . . I lack the talent . . . he has all the papers, all the documents . . .

OLD WOMAN [*echo*]: He has all the documents . . .

OLD MAN: A little patience, Sire, I beg of you . . . he should be coming.

OLD WOMAN: He should be coming in a moment.

OLD MAN [*so that the Emperor will not grow impatient*]: Your Majesty, hear me, a long time ago I had the revelation . . . I was forty years old . . . I say this also to you, ladies and gentlemen . . . one evening, after supper, as was our custom, before going to bed, I seated myself on my father's knees . . . my mustaches were longer than his and more pointed . . . I had more hair on my chest . . . my hair was graying already, but his was still brown . . . There were some guests, grownups, sitting at table, who began to laugh, laugh.

OLD WOMAN [*echo*]: Laugh . . . laugh . . .

OLD MAN: I'm not joking, I told them, I love my papa very much. Someone replied: It is midnight, a child shouldn't stay up so late. If you don't go beddy-bye, then you're no longer a kid. But I'd still not have believed them if they hadn't addressed me as an adult.

OLD WOMAN [*echo*]: An adult.

OLD MAN: Instead of as a child . . .

OLD WOMAN [*echo*]: A child.

OLD MAN: Nevertheless, I thought to myself, I'm not married. Hence, I'm still a child. They married me off right then, expressly to prove the contrary to me . . . Fortunately, my wife has been both father and mother to me . . .

OLD WOMAN: The Orator should be here, Your Majesty . . .

OLD MAN: The Orator will come.

OLD WOMAN: He will come.

OLD MAN: He will come.

OLD WOMAN: He will come.

OLD MAN: He will come.

OLD WOMAN: He will come.

OLD MAN: He will come, he will come.

OLD WOMAN: He will come, he will come.

OLD MAN: He will come.

OLD WOMAN: He is coming.

OLD MAN: He is coming.

OLD WOMAN: He is coming, he is here.

OLD MAN: He is coming, he is here.

OLD WOMAN: He is coming, he is here.

OLD MAN AND OLD WOMAN: He is here . . .

OLD WOMAN: Here he is!

[*Silence; all movement stops. Petrified, the two old people stare at door No. 5; this immobility lasts rather long—about thirty seconds; very slowly, very slowly the door opens wide, silently; then the Orator appears. He is a real person. He's a typical painter or poet of the nineteenth century; he wears a large black felt hat with a wide brim, loosely tied bow tie, artist's blouse, mustache and goatee, very histrionic in manner, conceited; just as the invisible people must be as real as possible, the Orator must appear unreal. He goes along the wall to the right, gliding, softly, to upstage center, in front of the main door, without turning his head to right or left; he passes close by the Old Woman without appearing to notice her, not even when the Old Woman touches his arm in order to assure herself that he exists. It is at this moment that the Old Woman says: "Here he is!"*]

OLD MAN: Here he is!

OLD WOMAN [*following the Orator with her eyes and continuing to stare at him*]: It's really he, he exists. In flesh and blood.

OLD MAN [*following him with his eyes*]: He exists. It's really he. This is not a dream!

OLD WOMAN: This is not a dream, I told you so.

[*The Old Man clasps his hands, lifts his eyes to heaven; he exults silently. The Orator, having reached upstage center, lifts his hat, bends forward in silence, saluting the invisible Emperor with his hat with a Musketeer's flourish and somewhat like an automaton. At this moment*:]

OLD MAN: Your Majesty . . . May I present to you, the Orator . . .

OLD WOMAN: It is he!

[*Then the Orator puts his hat back on his head and mounts the dais from which he looks down on the invisible crowd on the stage and at the chairs; he freezes in a solemn pose.*]

OLD MAN [*to the invisible crowd*]: You may ask him for autographs. [*Automatically, silently, the Orator signs and distributes numberless autographs. The Old Man during this time lifts his eyes again to heaven, clasping his hands, and exultantly says*:] No man, in his lifetime, could hope for more . . .

OLD WOMAN [*echo*]: No man could hope for more.

OLD MAN [*to the invisible crowd*]: And now, with the permission of Your Majesty, I will address myself to all of you, ladies, young ladies, gentlemen, little children, dear colleagues, dear compatriots, Your Honor the President, dear comrades in arms . . .

OLD WOMAN [*echo*]: And little children . . . dren . . . dren . . .

OLD MAN: I address myself to all of you, without distinction of age, sex, civil status, social rank, or business, to thank you, with all my heart.

OLD WOMAN [*echo*]: To thank you . . .

OLD MAN: As well as the Orator . . . cordially, for having come in such large numbers . . . silence, gentlemen! . . .

OLD WOMAN [*echo*]: . . . Silence, gentlemen . . .

OLD MAN: I address my thanks also to those who have made possible the meeting this evening, to the organizers . . .

OLD WOMAN: Bravo!

[*Meanwhile, the Orator on the dais remains solemn, immobile, except for his hand, which signs autographs automatically.*]

OLD MAN: To the owners of this building, to the architect, to the masons who were kind enough to erect these walls! . . .

OLD WOMAN [*echo*]: . . . walls . . .

OLD MAN: To all those who've dug the foundations . . . Silence, ladies and gentlemen . . .

OLD WOMAN: . . . 'adies and gentlemen . . .

OLD MAN: Last but not least I address my warmest thanks to the cabinet-makers who have made these chairs on which you have been able to sit, to the master carpenter . . .

OLD WOMAN [*echo*]: . . . penter . . .

OLD MAN: . . . Who made the armchair in which Your Majesty is sinking so softly, which does not prevent you, nevertheless, from maintaining a firm and manly attitude . . . Thanks again to all the technicians, machinists, electrocutioners . . .

OLD WOMAN [*echoing*:] . . . cutioners . . . cutioners . . .

OLD MAN: . . . To the paper manufacturers and the printers, proofreaders, editors to whom we owe the programs, so charmingly decorated, to the universal solidarity of all men, thanks, thanks, to our country, to the State [*He turns toward where the Emperor is sitting*:] whose helm Your Majesty directs with the skill of a true pilot . . . thanks to the usher . . .

OLD WOMAN [*echo*:] . . . usher . . . rusher . . .

OLD MAN [*pointing to the Old Woman*]: Hawker of Eskimo pies and programs . . .

OLD WOMAN [*echo*]: . . . grams . . .

OLD MAN: . . . My wife, my helpmeet . . . Semiramis! . . .

OLD WOMAN [*echo*]: . . . ife . . . meet . . . mis . . . [*Aside*:] The darling, he never forgets to give me credit.

OLD MAN: Thanks to all those who have given me their precious and expert, financial or moral support, thereby contributing to the overwhelming success of this evening's gathering . . . thanks again, thanks above all to our beloved sovereign, His Majesty the Emperor . . .

OLD WOMAN [*echo*]: . . . jesty the Emperor . . .

OLD MAN [*in a total silence*]: . . . A little silence . . . Your Majesty . . .

OLD WOMAN [*echo*]: . . . jesty . . . jesty . . .

OLD MAN: Your Majesty, my wife and myself have nothing more to ask of life. Our existence can come to an end in this apotheosis . . . thanks be to heaven who has granted us such long and peaceful years . . . My life has been filled to overflowing. My mission is accomplished. I will not have lived in vain, since my message will be revealed to the world . . . [*Gesture towards the Orator, who does not perceive it; the Orator waves off requests for autographs, very dignified and firm.*] To the world, or rather to what is left of it! [*Wide gesture toward the invisible crowd.*] To you, ladies and gentlemen, and dear comrades, who are all that is left from humanity, but with such leftovers one can still make a very good soup . . . Orator, friend . . . [*The Orator looks in another direction.*] If I have been long unrecognized, underestimated by my contemporaries, it is because it had to be . . . [*The Old Woman sobs.*] What matters all that now when I am leaving to you, to you, my dear Orator and friend [*The Orator rejects a new request for an autograph, then takes an indifferent pose, looking in all directions.*] . . . the responsibility of radiating upon posterity the light of my mind . . . thus making known to the universe my philosophy. Neglect none of the details of my private life, some laughable, some painful or heartwarming, of my tastes, my amusing gluttony . . . tell everything . . . speak of my helpmeet . . . [*The Old Woman redoubles her sobs.*] . . . of the way she prepared those marvelous little Turkish pies, of her potted rabbit à la Normandabbit . . . speak of Berry, my native province . . . I count on you, great master and Orator . . . as for me and my faithful helpmeet, after our long years of labor in behalf of the progress of humanity during which we fought the good fight, nothing remains for us but to withdraw . . . immediately, in order to make the supreme sacrifice which no one demands of us but which we will carry out even so . . .

OLD WOMAN [*sobbing*]: Yes, yes, let's die in full glory . . . let's die in order to become a legend . . . At least, they'll name a street after us . . .

OLD MAN [*to Old Woman*]: O my faithful helpmeet! . . . you who have believed in me, unfailingly, during a whole century, who have never left me, never . . . alas, today, at this supreme moment, the crowd pitilessly separates us . . .

> Above all I had hoped
> that together we might lie
> with all our bones together
> within the selfsame skin
> within the same sepulchre
> and that the same worms
> might share our old flesh
> that we might rot together . . .

OLD WOMAN: . . . Rot together . . .

OLD MAN: Alas! . . .alas! . . .

OLD WOMAN: Alas! . . . alas! . . .

OLD MAN: . . . Our corpses will fall far from each other, and we will rot in an aquatic solitude . . . Don't pity us over much.

OLD WOMAN: What will be, will be!

OLD MAN: We shall not be forgotten. The eternal Emperor will remember us, always.

OLD WOMAN [*echo*]: Always.

OLD MAN: We will leave some traces, for we are people and not cities.

OLD MAN AND OLD WOMAN [*together*]: We will have a street named after us.

OLD MAN: Let us be united in time and in eternity, even if we are not together in space, as we were in adversity: let us die at the same moment . . . [*To the Orator, who is impassive, immobile*:] One last time . . . I place my trust in you . . . I count on you. You will tell all . . . bequeath my message . . . [*To the Emperor*:] If Your Majesty will excuse me . . . Farewell to all. Farewell, Semiramis.

OLD WOMAN: Farewell to all! . . . Farewell, my darling!

OLD MAN: Long live the Emperor!

[*He throws confetti and paper streamers on the invisible Emperor; we hear fanfares; bright lights like fireworks.*]

OLD WOMAN: Long live the Emperor!

[*Confetti and streamers thrown in the direction of the Emperor, then on the immobile and impassive Orator, and on the empty chairs.*]

OLD MAN [*same business*]: Long live the Emperor!

OLD WOMAN [*same business*]: Long live the Emperor!

[*The Old Woman and Old Man at the same moment throw themselves out the windows, shouting "Long Live the Emperor." Sudden silence; no more fireworks; we hear an "Ah" from both sides of the stage, the sea-green noises of bodies falling into the water. The light coming through the main door and the windows has disappeared; there remains only a weak light as at the beginning of the play; the darkened windows remain wide open, their curtains floating on the wind.*]

ORATOR [*he has remained immobile and impassive during the scene of the double suicide, and now, after several moments, he decides to speak. He faces the rows of empty chairs; he makes the invisible crowd understand that he is deaf and dumb; he makes the signs of a deafmute; desperate efforts to make himself understood; then he coughs, groans, utters the gutteral sounds of a mute*]: He, mme, mm, mm. Ju, gou, hou, hou. Heu, heu, gu gou, gueue.

[*Helpless, he lets his arms fall down alongside his body; suddenly, his face lights up, he has an idea, he turns toward the blackboard, he takes a piece of chalk out of his pocket, and writes, in large capitals*:

ANGELFOOD

then:

NNAA NNM NWNWNW V

He turns around again, towards the invisible crowd on the stage, and points with his finger to what he's written on the blackboard.]

ORATOR: Mmm, Mmm, Gueue, Gou, Gu. Mmm, Mmm, Mmm, Mmm.

[*Then, not satisfied, with abrupt gestures he wipes out the chalk letters, and replaces them with others, among which we can make out, still in large capitals*:

ΛADIEU ΛDIEU ΛPΛ

Again, the Orator turns around to face the crowd; he smiles, questions, with an air of hoping that he's been understood, of having said something; he indicates to the empty chairs what he's just written. He remains immobile for a few seconds, rather satisfied and a little solemn; but then, faced with the absence of the hoped for reaction, little by little his smile disappears, his face darkens; he waits another moment; suddenly he bows petulantly, brusquely, descends from the dais; he goes toward the main door upstage center, gliding like a ghost; before exiting through this door, he bows ceremoniously again to the rows of empty chairs, to the invisible Emperor. The stage remains empty with only the chairs, the dais, the floor covered with streamers and confetti. The main door is wide open onto darkness.

We hear for the first time the human noises of the invisible crowd; these are bursts of laughter, murmurs, shh's, ironical coughs; weak at the beginning, these noises grow louder, then, again, progressively they become weaker. All this should last long enough for the audience—the real and visible audience—to leave with this ending firmly impressed on its mind. The curtain falls very slowly.]

April–June, 1951

* In the original production the curtain fell on the mumblings of the mute Orator. The blackboard was not used.